SAVE THE SWAMP

SAVE THE SWAMP

CAREER GUIDEBOOK FOR BUDDING BUREAUCRATS

THOMAS L. KRANNAWITTER, PH.D.

SPEAKEASY *Ideas*

ISBN: 978-0-99609-282-1

Printed in the United States of America
First Printing: 2017
20 19 18 17 16   5 4 3 2 1

Published by Speakeasy Ideas
To order, visit www.speakeasyideas.com

.

satire /**sat**-ahyuh r/

n.

A poem, novel, film, or other work of art that uses humor, irony, exaggeration, or ridicule to expose and criticize prevailing foolishness, esp. as a form of social or political commentary.

—*Oxford English Dictionary*

CONTENTS

INCENTIVES FOR A BUREAUCRAT

PRIVACY: THE DEVIL'S DEN

FOREWORD

By Philbert C. Dempster, J.D., M.P.A.[1]

T he United States was built on public service. From our second-rate system of public roads, to our usually reliable grid of electricity (except for brown-outs and black-outs), to modern medicine, to the Internet, and much more, the modern way of life enjoyed by hundreds of millions of Americans owes its existence almost entirely to the career federal workforce in Washington, D.C., and the millions of civil servants in government bureaus, offices, agencies, and cubicles across the nation. And they are being attacked, politically.

That's why there's no more important book for our time than Dr. Thomas Krannawitter's *Save the Swamp: Career Guidebook for Budding Bureaucrats.* We, the men, women, and other-gendered people of our civil service, need a clearly written guide for navigating the many obstacles in government bureaucracies and regulatory agencies as we advance our careers. We also need insights and tactical instruction to help our fellow bureaucrats

---

[1] Philbert C. Dempster is the Senior Assistant Deputy Director of Monitoring and Tracking within the Office of Diversity Management and Equal Opportunity, United States Department of Regulatory Agencies. He holds a Juris Doctorate and a Master's Degree in Public Administration.

identify, understand, and defeat our political opponents. This book provides precisely those kinds of lessons not found in typical public administration textbooks or classes.

Vocal conservative critics, cranks, and naysayers hold sway in certain media outlets and "red" states. They stand to ruin everything bureaucrats have built. They are not merely extremists, they're the most deplorable kind of extremists: right-wingers. The problem is that these conservative "deplorables" are finding friends in high places. Some politicians, including President Trump, talk openly about "draining the swamp." One member of Congress, Representative Ken Buck, went so far as to write a book rudely titled *Drain the Swamp*.

When extremist politicians use that phrase, "drain the swamp," let's be clear about whom they are talking: honest, hard-working, patriotic men, women, and trans-gendered people—including people of the LGBTQQI community and others to whom we cannot refer because they find any reference offensive and in violation of their civil service anti-discrimination rights—who are unelected government employees. These person-beings are loyal and reliable. They often show up for work, except when they are excused according to the rules and regulations in the *United States Government Dismissal and Closing Procedures* manual, of course. These bureaucrats are the ones making America great.

The "swamp" doesn't need to be drained. It needs to be *saved*. Saving the swamp means saving the American way of life and everything Americans hold dear, from clean water and air, to quality public education, to equal opportunities for people of all sexual orientations in private businesses big and small, to socialized medicine, to the beautiful national parks and forests in the United States, all of which could not and would not exist without bureaucrats and regulators.

Saving the swamp means inspiring more Americans to devote themselves to government careers, protecting others from themselves and their own careless choices. We need more Americans willing to control the property and businesses of others with government force. Saving the swamp requires some people showing they care by voting to spend other people's money on government programs and projects. We also need armies of bureaucrats to redistribute that money to those who voted for those programs and projects and the crony politicians who created them. In short, saving the swamp is the most important thing for Americans who want to see the United States go forward and make real progress into the future.

A recent article in *Government Executive* magazine quoted Bill Valdez, president of the Senior Executives Association and a former United States Energy Department employee with decades of bureaucratic experience: "The premise that career employees are responsible for the proliferation of regulations in [modern government] is incorrect, because no regulations are developed without the approval of the political leadership."[2] Mr. Valdez is right. Bureaucratic regulators are not responsible for the proliferation of regulations. How could they be?

Many public employee unions, including the American Federation of Government and the National Active and Retired Federal Employees Association, both of which are proud partners with (and contributors to) the members of Congress who vote routinely to increase my salary, are offended by suggestions that career bureaucrats are a problem. And rightly so. If politicians and citizens openly criticize bureaucrats, it might, in the words of one government expert in human resources management, "hurt federal recruitment and retention of talented employees as well as the overall morale of the government workforce." That's troubling. And scary. Imagine the damage that would result if the number of Americans interested in becoming career bureaucrats drops *and* the already low standards of government employee morale became even lower.

The United States will only be as good as the bureaucrats who staff the many government agencies, offices, and departments at the local, county, state, and national levels. The question is: How do we get the best Americans interested in government careers when agitators are

---

[2] References and citations can be found online at speakeasyideas.com/swamp

mocking those who work in government and haters are organizing to scale back the bureaucratic-regulatory state?

We all know that in the progressive, modern United States, many Americans likely will not work at all. They'll produce nothing that others value. They are people who exercise their right not to be dehumanized by the machinery of capitalism. That's okay, so long as we have adequate numbers of qualified, certified, licensed bureaucrats who can redistribute other people's property to them in the form of entitlements while providing the therapy they need to cope with idleness.

Other Americans might be naïve enough to work for a private sector business, and a greedy few will try to start new businesses on their own. That, too, is okay so long as we have adequate numbers of qualified, certified, licensed regulators to watch over those businesses and tell them what to do and how to do it, including how employees will be treated, how much they'll be paid, and what prices for products and services are fair.

As a truly brilliant, male-identifying, African-American United States President remarked, "if you've been successful, you didn't get there on your own" because "if you've got a business, you didn't build that—someone else made that happen." Success in business has little to do with the sweat, creativity, tireless effort, risk, and strategic choices of business owners. Businesses succeed not because they are innovative, inventive, or more efficient than their competitors. They succeed because of the infrastructure provided by government. In particular, businesses succeed when they are guided by government experts, regulators, and bureaucrats who take away what businesses don't need while providing what businesses do need. Without bureaucratic oversight, businesses fuel social anarchy, injustice, and unbridled greed. Without strict regulations, business owners use helpless government officials to advance their selfish business interests.

The good news is that government bureaucracy in the United States—local, state, and federal—has become so big, and controls so much wealth produced by Americans, that the bureaucracy itself has become the biggest interest group in American politics. Government is no longer limited to representing the interests and protecting the individual rights of private citizens. Today, those in government stay busy representing the interests of bureaucrats. Increasingly, government represents the interests of government. That's a sign of the real progress we've made in recent decades. We want to keep building upon it.

Let's make sure government keeps growing and crowds out the interests of private citizens, private business owners, private activists, and anyone else who's not part of government. Nothing but corruption happens when the greedy private interests of greedy private citizens have a voice inside government. Let's silence those who object to our plans or raise too many questions about our purposes. And let's not stop until the only voices inside government are the voices of government interests, government employee unions, politicians, regulators, and bureaucrats. First Amendment free speech was created by government. It's enforced by government. It should be limited to those in government. Why protect the voices and free speech of haters who want to criticize the important work being done by government?

Let's save the swamp by expanding it. We need to fill it with more resources and more regulators for the future. In short, we need you. If you make the important choice to enter public service and begin a career as a bureaucrat, you will find great assistance navigating the complex world of government agencies, moving your career up the ladder of success and power, and learning how to dismiss and ridicule those who challenge government regulatory power, with the book you are now reading. Good luck. And bless you, in a way not intended to be offensive or to discriminate in favor of or against any particular religion or irreligion.

GETTING STARTED

T his book is a career guide for Americans who are serving their country right now as distinguished civil servants, working inside the thousands of regulatory agencies, bureaus, and other government offices staffed by unelected government employees. It's also a book for American students, and those who are not yet employed professionally, but who dream of someday working inside a cubicle at the Office of Community Planning and Development, the Consumer Safety Products Commission, the Bureau of Land Management, the Federal Communications Commission, or some other exalted government ministry.

This is *not* a book for Americans whose ambition is to accept the relatively transparent responsibility of becoming an elected member of government, such as a Congressperson, President of the United States, or a governor or state legislator. The book you are holding in your hands (or viewing on a screen, or listening to) is for the many millions who either are among, or want to join, the nameless, faceless, virtually anonymous unelected career bureaucrats who wield far more power over American citizens than most people know. This is the *Career Guidebook for Budding Bureaucrats.*

FINDING YOUR PLACE WITHIN THE BUREAUCRACY

Today, at the federal level alone, the United States government includes 15 executive branch "departments." Virtually all federal regulatory and administrative agencies—which number in the hundreds, and employ directly around 3 million non-military, unelected, civil service bureaucrats—fall under the authority of one of these departments. These departments are, in the chronological order in which they were created:

1. Department of State
2. Department of the Treasury
3. Department of Justice
4. Department of the Interior
5. Department of Agriculture
6. Department of Commerce
7. Department of Labor
8. Department of Defense
9. Department of Health & Human Services
10. Department of Housing & Urban Development
11. Department of Transportation
12. Department of Energy
13. Department of Education
14. Department of Veterans Affairs
15. Department of Homeland Security

Some of these departments (such as the Department of Defense) were formed by combining government agencies, or by splitting some apart (such as Labor and Commerce). Congress created all of these departments by statutory laws, which means only Congress can dismantle, dissolve, restructure, or repurpose them. Congress created 10 of these 15 departments just within the past century as part of the progressive expansion of government.

Not all unelected bureaucrats work for the federal government. Many work at the state, county, or local levels of government. In many states, for example, K-12 public education systems employ more non-teaching bureaucrats than teachers. The realm of public higher education, including colleges and universities at the undergraduate and graduate levels, has also seen a spike in the rate of hiring non-teaching bureaucrats that has dwarfed increases in the numbers of students and professors, combined.

Add to the numbers of federal civil service employees the many regulators, inspectors, administrators, clerks, and bureaucrats of all kinds employed by state, county, and local governments, and the total balloons to between 20 and 25 million Americans who work for government at some level. To put this in perspective: Approximately twice as many Americans are employed by government today—as unelected bureaucrats—as are employed by all manufacturing companies added together.

While these numbers do not include those serving in the United States military, many government bureaucracies are looking increasingly like commando units. For example, there are now more heavily armed, non-military, unelected bureaucrats than there are active United States Marines. IRS agents carry AR-15 military rifles. Bureaucrats at Health and Human Services receive combat training from Army Special Forces contractors. The Department of Veterans Affairs, alone, has approximately 4,000 armed employees.

These government agencies and more, including the Small Business Administration, Social Security Administration, National Oceanic and Atmospheric Administration, Education Department, Energy Department, Bureau of Engraving and Printing, and National Institute of Standards and Technology, have spent hundreds of millions of dollars purchasing military grade weapons, guns, and many millions of rounds of ammunition. Bureaucrats are preparing to enforce regulations against American citizens as if they're preparing for war.

There's more. Much government work is performed by government contractors and government grant recipients—from weapons developers to "non-profit," tax-exempt charities, to big government political advocates, to organizations that launder government money and return it to politicians who vote reliably in support of more bureaucracy, more bureaucrats, and bigger government budgets. Often, taxpayers fund most or all of the work of these contractors and charitable grantees.

If we add the many contractors and charitable organizations that receive taxpayer-funding to all the Americans employed directly by the government at the federal, state, county, and local levels, we find that a whopping 19% of employed Americans work for government in one way or another, directly or indirectly. That's right: Approximately one out of every five working Americans gets their paycheck from taxpayers and government programs. Which is great news for budding bureaucrats. It almost certainly means a place can be found for you.

As the reach of government power has grown and extended into virtually all areas of life, the losers are those who think small and act small, like small business owners and individual citizens. The winners are those who think big, and act big, especially big businesses, big public employee unions, and proponents of big government. Big bureaucracies have become commonplace, and new ones are added every year. The Patient Protection and Affordable Health Care Act, as just one recent example, created more than 150 new bureaucratic boards, commissions, programs, and government offices.

Even elected politicians are coming to look more and more like lifetime career bureaucrats. More than 90% of the members of Congress have won re-election at least once, despite American approval ratings of Congress hovering around 15%, and occasionally dipping to 10%

or lower. Members of Congress are now far more likely to retire (with a full government pension) or die in office from old age than to be voted out of office.

On the rare occasion that a politician leaves Congress, he or she almost immediately goes to work as a lobbyist in Washington, D.C., helping big crony businesses get favors from the big government bureaucracies and programs the former politician helped to create or expand. This explains why seven of the ten wealthiest counties in the United States are now in the Washington, D.C. metropolitan area, and why D.C. now has the highest rates of fine-wine consumption in the country. Life is good for bureaucrats, at least those who learn the ways of the bureaucracy.

THE IMPORTANT WORK WAITING FOR YOU

Each of these departments, agencies, offices, boards, and commissions, at all levels of government, is important, each in its own way. From local building inspectors and federal forest campground monitors, to the directors, deputy directors, and assistant deputy directors of federal agencies—all fit together to form the large, modern administrative-bureaucratic state. The administrative-bureaucratic state adds intelligence, expertise, and the authority of science to the laws, regulations, programs, and policies that command how Americans run their businesses, raise their children, use their property, worship inside their churches, participate in elections, and live their lives. Which is good for all of us.

The laws and regulations enforced by bureaucrats keep Americans safe from each other and from themselves. Government programs and policies supply many citizens (and non-citizens) with many things they've never produced, earned, or purchased but to which they have an unchallengeable right. In that way, modern American laws, regulations, and programs, and the bureaucrats who enforce them, are necessary, good, and immeasurably beneficial, which is why it's foolish for anyone to question, much less criticize, much less oppose any of them. The modern administrative-bureaucratic state was designed by reason. It is reason. Any opposition to the modern administrative-bureaucratic state, therefore, must be irrational. Sadly, that does not mean there is no opposition.

But let's not drift into negativity or controversy. Let's focus on the positive. If your ambition is to become a bureaucrat, or if you're already a bureaucratic and you're looking to climb the ladder of success and shore up the agency that's now the home of your career, then congratulations! And, thank you!

As you prepare to tell Americans how to live their lives, run their businesses, and raise their kids, please know that your fellow citizens (and non-citizens) are in your debt. Even if they don't acknowledge it. Most people don't make good choices on their own, so they should appreciate the regulatory guidance and supervision you provide, whether they admit how much they owe you or not.

We all know it, right? It's the truth. That's why the work you do as a bureaucrat is so valuable to your fellow citizens, even though most of them don't want to pay for your work. Strangely, the most vocal advocates for more government programs and bureaucrats try any way they can to avoid paying for them. But never mind common sense economic concepts such as value measured by how much people are willing to pay. That doesn't matter for you. You live according to the motto of the bureaucratic spirit: Force others to follow regulations in spite of common sense.

You know in your heart of hearts that you want to help people. That's why you're going to spend the next 30 years or so slaving inside a cubicle in a government office building and enforcing government regulations. Yours is a labor of sacrifice, truth be told, and people ought to thank you for all you are giving up to serve them. Pay no attention to the price tag some people might attempt to put on your work. Unless it happens to be members of Congress who want to increase the price you get paid for your work. So they can raise taxes on others to pay for it. That's always worth paying attention to.

A PRACTICAL GUIDE

As a bureaucrat looking to build a long and satisfying professional career inside a government office or agency, you'll want to pay close attention to the ways elected politicians think about you and the work you do and the government office or agency of which you are part. In most cases, elected politicians have great influence over your budget, so you'll want to have a good relationship with them when you go to request more funding. (See, you're getting practical professional advice already and you're only in the first chapter.)

Which brings us to the purpose of this book. As the subtitle suggests, this is emphatically a *career guide* for budding bureaucrats. It's not a history of the modern administrative-bureaucratic state. It's not a treatise of political philosophy. It's not academic gibberish. It doesn't examine any particular regulations or regulatory agencies or government bureaucracies. This is no narrow policy study. Hordes of policy wonks crank out mountains of white papers on all kinds of laws, programs, and regulations, most of which no one reads, so why repeat the ignored work they've already done?

Rather, this is an eminently practical book filled with helpful advice. This book presents and clarifies the two most critical success factors for your career. Mastering both of these success factors is essential for you to thrive within a modern bureaucracy. In some ways, it's essential for your very survival as an unelected government professional. For the sake of your self-interest and the interests of your family and friends, including crony friends, you must learn both.

SUCCESS FACTOR ONE: SWIMMING IN THE SWAMP

The first of the two success factors is understanding and learning to use the special perks, privileges, and power that come with the government ID dangling around your neck. After finishing this book, you'll be able to leverage your position within government for many kinds of personal and professional benefits.

As a bureaucrat, you don't merely want to be in the swamp. You want to know how to swim in the swamp. You want to master the bureaucratic versions of the backstroke, breaststroke, sidestroke, and butterfly so that you can slide through the muck, the slime, and the goo with ease. Think of this book as your swamp swimming trainer.

In the coming chapters, you'll learn the kind of insider, real-life advice that one typically does not receive in college or graduate school. This book reveals secrets that you need to know (but which few are even willing to whisper) if you want to achieve success as a bureaucrat. Many long-time bureaucrats who now wield power within the administrative-bureaucratic state are reluctant to share these insider secrets—mainly because they don't want competition. They're bureaucrats, after all, so why would they want competition?

But you don't need to rely on them for education and tips to get ahead within government agencies so long as you study *Save the Swamp* with care and attention, and practice the real-life bureaucratic skills and strategies offered in these pages.

SUCCESS FACTOR TWO: SAVING THE SWAMP

The second of the success factors is relatively new because it involves responding to a new political threat to the swamp of modern government bureaucracies. It's a factor of professional survival. It's a matter of protecting the very bureaucracy where you work. It's knowing how to recognize, refute, mock, and defeat those people, usually lurking in dark corners of modern American conservative culture, who raise objections and make arguments against bureaucracies and regulatory agencies.

A movement currently gaining momentum presents a grave threat to the unelected, bureaucratic institutions of modern government in the United States and to the bureaucrats who make lifelong careers within them. Make no mistake, this movement poses a formidable political and professional threat to you, personally. If the extremism of this movement prevails, we could see a return to the old-fashioned, obsolete style of limited government that prevailed before progressives ballooned the size and power of the bureaucracy that provides your livelihood, your self-esteem, and, of course, your power over others.

There are two basic kinds of activists in this modern anti-government, anti-bureaucracy movement, and you would be wise to consider both as your enemies. One group opposes you for serious, principled, Constitutional reasons. They present arguments connected to free market economics, the political theory of the American Founding, the rule of law, and the Constitution, as well as general concerns regarding human flourishing and its connection to human freedom. They are attempting to build political coalitions upon these ideas, all for the purpose of scaling back and even dismantling some of the administrative-regulatory bureaucracies where you and your fellow bureaucrats work. They want to take power away from you.

The other group, who are equally your enemies, are perhaps best described as populists. They oppose you less for intellectual or principled reasons, and more because they are cheerleaders for politicians who disparage big, bloated, wasteful government. These partisan populists typically have not studied the Constitution, economics, or related subjects. Instead, they are inspired by undefined, vague, simplistic rallying cries like *Make America Great Again!* and *Drain the Swamp!* Populists jump on the bandwagon of whatever is popular, and recently it's become popular to attack bureaucrats and regulators.

For you and the future of your bureaucratic career, these populists matter. They can vote. If they vote in sufficient numbers for politicians who disparage the good work you and your cohorts do, those politicians might actually start scaling back and even dismantling some of the administrative-regulatory bureaucracies just to boost their popularity and increase power for themselves. You and your fellow bureaucrats don't want to become scapegoats blamed by political demagogues as America's biggest problem.

Triumphing over both of these groups, principled Constitutionalists *and* populists, is the second purpose for this career guide for bureaucrats and regulators. You need to learn not only the personal and professional skills for swimming in the swamp, but also the political skills necessary for saving the swamp. And saving the swam requires defeating critics of the swamp.

To begin, you must know thy enemy. You need to be able to recognize and identify the people who form this new threat to the modern administrative-bureaucratic state. You should learn how they think and why they pursue their extremist goals. If you are to unravel and refute their assertions, or, even better, mock and ridicule them into irrelevance and harass them into silence, then you'll need to understand their arguments. You should know the most vulnerable parts of their conservative propaganda and the weakest links in their chain of reactionary, fear-induced and fear-inducing arguments.

Accordingly, this career guide for bureaucrats will occasionally take some slight detours and explain the philosophy of old-fashioned Constitutionalism—an ancient way of thinking that continues to haunt the hallways of conservative think tanks and schools of Constitutional government—while explaining the relevance of that philosophy and the real threat it poses for your future. It might seem strange to revisit ancient Constitutional ideas and principles of political theory that were discarded by progressive Americans decades ago, but many of your conservative critics continue to cling to those old prejudices from the American Founding. Apparently, no one told your critics that their ideas are outdated. Which is why you need to be familiar with those ideas, silly as they might be.

This guide will also identify the pithy slogans and allegedly pro-freedom, often irrational, talking points that fill populists with enthusiasm at political rallies and on social media. Nothing stirs populists like unsubstantiated memes floating around Facebook or fake news assertions at mob meetings. Principled, pro-freedom, pro-Constitution, anti-bureaucracy arguments can be refuted. Pithy slogans, however, should be mocked. This career guide will help you become better at both.

PREPARATION

As you prepare for your long, long career in public service, you need to demonstrate to other bureaucrats that you've been properly educated. The best way to do that is by obtaining a degree from an accredited college or university. The good news for bureaucrats and regulators is that many jobs in government do not require any particular technical skills. You don't actually need to know how to do something, build something, or repair something. You certainly don't need to be inventive, innovative, or entrepreneurial because invention, innovation, and entrepreneurism are not the purposes of the modern administrative-bureaucratic state. Controlling those who invent and innovate in entrepreneurial efforts, is.

Perhaps most important, you need no education in what used to be called the classical liberal arts. At best, classical education is *b-o-r-i-n-g*. At worst, it's oppressive and insulting.

Seriously, can you imagine someone actually believing that Socrates or Shakespeare, Cicero or Locke, could illuminate the path that we today ought to follow? What do they know about our challenges, interests, or agendas? What do they know about *anything* other than being white, being homophobic, being misogynistic, being colonizers, being warmongers? What could they possibly know about human nature? How could studying old books and the authors who wrote them make us feel good about ourselves and what we are advocating right now, right here, in this moment?

Classical liberal arts are a silly and sad form of education. The liberal arts should come with trigger warnings because few decent, modern progressive people are prepared to confront the racist, bigoted throwbacks from the past who cared nothing for the plight of the poor and even less for the climatological health of Mother Earth.

For those who want careers as bureaucrats, study whatever you want, but it's best to stay away from classical liberal arts education. And don't worry about acquiring any technical skills or practical expertise. Above all, study the subjects that make you feel good:

- *Fourth-Wave Feminism?* That's a great major to have in college.
- *Queer Theory?* Not at all gay.
- *White Oppression Disguised as Multicultural Studies?* What could be more important?
- *Government Control Over the Global Climate?* Tailored for the bureaucratic soul.
- *Progressive Activism Parading as Political Science?* Weren't all the modern social sciences invented to promote activism and advocacy for progressive, big government causes?
- *Sociology Solutions for the Problems Created by the Welfare State?* We all should learn how government

programs can cure the social pathologies caused by government programs.

It's useful to remember when selecting a college major that while technical skills are not necessary for a long and successful career as a bureaucrat, it is important to understand the science of victimhood espoused by many elected politicians (who have the power to expand budgets for bureaucratic government agencies). The more you can focus your college studies on historically victimized groups and the politics of envy, rage, and revenge, the more you will have in common with the progressive elected officials who will be looking to you, as an unelected bureaucrat, for favors in exchange for the increased funding you want.

Further, if you want to deepen your educational bona fides among progressive bureaucrats, make sure you participate in plenty of college campus protests, riots, sit-ins, and walk-outs. Your open displays of being easily offended as a student will be good practice. Later in your bureaucratic career, being easily offended will help you get more of what you demand, including increased budgets and more power for the government office where you work.

It's important that you get some kind of university degree, however. It can be virtually any degree, but you'll likely need an academic diploma to gain respect and employment within the halls of government bureaus and regulatory agencies. The people who created government bureaus and regulatory agencies, after all, were the people who created and continue to regulate and monitor the modern university system. It is no exaggeration to suggest that the whole purpose of the modern university system is to produce the next generation of progressives who will staff the regulatory agencies within the modern adminis-trative-bureaucratic state. Being counted among the best educated, and being counted among bureaucrats, is the same thing in the modern administrative-bureaucratic state. That's why the first step in becoming a successful bureaucrat is to get the basic educational credential needed by any bureaucrat: a university degree.

PLAN OF THE BOOK

In addition to this introductory "Getting Started" section and the concluding "Important Work Ahead," this career guidebook consists of 18 short chapters. The book focuses on the essential, distilled lessons that you most need to land a job within a government bureau and build a growing and successful career as a civil servant, all while helping to defeat and destroy the political critics of big government, regulations, and bureaucracies.

This is a good place to offer a disclaimer regarding the writing style herein. This is a book for bureaucrats and regulators. Everyone knows that regulatory docu-ments are written in bureaucratese so that ordinary citizens cannot understand them, and therefore cannot understand how and why they're being regulated. But this career guidebook is different than most modern government documents. It has been written in clear, concise, sometimes entertaining prose, knowing that the typical bureaucrat is smarter and savvier than the typical citizen. Bureaucrats deserve a reading experience that reflects their superior intelligence and sophistication. And this book aims for the high standards of excellence fitting for lifetime government employees. In addition, bureaucrats spend a lifetime reading unreadable bureaucratic forms, documents, policies, and regulations, so this book is meant to offer a little reprieve from the ordinary. In more ways than one.

For those interested in the stories, data, and references cited in each chapter, you'll find an online bibliography for *Save the Swamp* at speakeasyideas.com/swamp. You will also find additional resources that will help you and others deepen your understanding of regulatory agencies and bureaucracies in the United States today.

Get ready. Get set. Prepare to take notes. The information is going to come fast and furiously. Each chapter is short and will take only a few minutes to read. You're the right person for a government agency. You have the bureaucratic interests and ambitions to rule others without being elected. You have the spirit for public service. You are the public spirit!

After reading this book, the world of bureaucratic power will be yours. You will choose who to control, from whom to take, and to whom to give. You will dictate when, in what circumstances, and with what resources to pursue the projects you choose. You will decide along the way which politicians need to be in your back pocket, and which citizen critics need to shut up or be shut down. This book shows the path to bureaucratic glory and power, because this is *Save the Swamp: Career Guidebook for Budding Bureaucrats.*

PART
I

WHAT IT MEANS

TO BE A BUREAUCRAT
AND THE TOOLS
AVAILABLE TO YOU

CHAPTER 1

REGULATIONS: YOUR DISTRUST AND SUSPICION EMPOWERED

T his chapter begins with one of the brief detours mentioned earlier. If you don't yet know, regulations will be indispensable to your career as a bureaucrat. Regulations are the main tool you will use to control the lives and property of citizens. It's important, therefore, that you understand the essence of regulations, the kind of thing regulations are.

To highlight just how radical and potentially powerful regulations are, let's first clarify what regulations are *not*. Regulations are not connected to the old, Constitutional form of government and laws that arose during the American Founding. In many respects, regulations are the opposite of that musty form of Constitutional government. So let's turn to the American Founders for a moment and learn their views on government power. Then we will come back to the subject of regulations and contrast it with the views of the Founders. The differences will be striking, and therefore memorable.

FREEDOMTRUST: PIE IN THE SKY

The signers of the 1776 Declaration of Independence concluded with a solemn and famous pledge: their lives, fortunes, and sacred honor. This was no small matter. What they were calling "revolution" was, from the British government's point of view, treason against the Crown and punishable by death.

But the American revolutionaries, including the Declaration signers and many others, stood strong together and launched the great American experiment in freedom and Constitutional self-government. That experiment required one indispensable ingredient, without which the American Revolution would have failed and the American Founding never would have happened: *trust*. In that regard, it is no exaggeration to suggest that the American Revolution and subsequent American Founding represented a kind of *freedomtrust*.

The pledge offered by the Declaration's signers, after all, was not a pledge to God. Nor was it a pledge to their fellow countrymen. Their pledge was to each other.

They knew, every one of them, that if any among them broke the trust when the going got tough—and the going was about to get very tough!—others would likely break it too, and the revolution would fail. Betraying their mutual trust would likely have meant that the revolutionaries would die in vain and the great experiment in freedom and self-government would have to wait for another time, another place, another people.

But the American revolutionaries honored their trust, at great cost in blood, money, and suffering. The (relative) freedom Americans have enjoyed over the past two and a half centuries is a legacy of the revolutionaries' remarkable loyalty to and trust in each other.

The theme of mutual civic trust runs throughout the literature of the American Founding. "Trust" was often used as a synonym for freedom and self-government. Freedom, after all, requires citizens who trust each other to govern themselves, raise their children as they see fit, run their private businesses as they please. Freedom requires citizens who trust each other to make their own choices in life, responsibly, and to enjoy the successes or suffer the consequences that follow. *Live and let live* is the attitude and way of life for free men and women, an attitude inseparable from mutual *trust*.

This reliance on mutual civic trust and the promise of wide realms of individual freedom led the Founders to design a Constitution that featured only a few powers, delegated to the government by the people, and directed at one supreme governmental goal: offering equal protection for the person and property of each citizen. They believed that free citizens, busy being productive in order to provide for themselves and their families, while trusting others to do the same, needed relatively little government and legal oversight over their homes, businesses, and lives. This is the origin of the chants for "limited government" and the "rule of law" we hear today from some conservative critics of big, modern, regulatory government.

The original United States Constitution was one of enumerated powers, meaning each branch of government was supposed to possess and exercise only the few, specified powers granted to it by "We The People," through the Constitution, and no other powers. The Founders designed the Constitution to function as a great check on those serving in government offices by prohibiting them from doing anything other than the few things authorized by the Constitution.

The Founding generation of Americans trusted one another as private citizens, to a large degree. At the same time, they did *not* trust those in government. At all. They had just finished a bloody, miserable, revolutionary war against centralized government power, after all. They understood all too well that government is the unique entity that can use legalized force against others, including controlling and confiscating people's property and restricting their freedom, all backed by law. (Government as the monopoly on legalized force is discussed more in Chapter 14.)

Americans, at the time of the Founding, understood that government is necessary and very dangerous. Always. Regarding questions of. how much power those in government should exercise and how much they should be trusted, Thomas Jefferson wrote in 1798, "let no more be heard of confidence in man, but rather bind him down from mischief by the chains of the Constitution." The general civic spirit of the American Founding was mutual trust and wide latitudes of mutual freedom among citizens coupled with distrust towards, and clear Constitutional limits on, those in positions of government power.

There is, unfortunately, and sadly, a fatal error in the American Founders' view of freedom. Namely, it doesn't work. It's a view based on high hopes that inspire great optimism and faith in humankind. *But. It. Just. Does. Not. Work.*

After all, what was one of the first things those allegedly trusting, free Americans did after they won independence from England? Those with white skin instituted new laws protecting themselves while enslaving those with black skin.

Those same allegedly trusting, free Americans then went on to create all kinds of businesses and corporate empires, milking money from the poor while selling all kinds of unregulated, unhealthy, and often dangerous products—including foods and medicines—to unsuspecting citizens. In other words, those allegedly free, trusting Americans used their freedom, almost immediately, to scam each other, hurt each other, and rip each other off. They betrayed their mutual trust as soon as they pronounced it.

Today, Americans continue to hurt each other in all kinds of ways. They lie. They cheat. They steal. They're fraudulent. They promise things they cannot deliver. They deceive customers. They price-gouge and overcharge for whatever they're selling, every chance they get. They care about making a profit, and little else. And everyone knows that those who desire to make a profit are the ones most eager to hurt, and least willing to help, others.

Americans are not good at parenting their own children. Child Protection Services agencies and related social work offices have more staff and deal with more cases of child abuse than ever, not fewer. Americans are not even good at taking care of themselves. Across the United States, rates of domestic abuse, sexual abuse, spousal abuse, drug abuse, alcohol abuse, and neglect are significantly higher than they were just a century ago.

DISTRUSTING THE UNTRUSTWORTHY

So this idea of the United States as some freedomtrust— the notion that individual freedom bound up with mutual civic trust among citizens justifies a limited Constitutional government that operates by the rule of a few laws—is pie-in-the-sky, fantastic, wishful nonsense. We simply cannot trust Americans to do the right thing, to provide for themselves and their families, to run their own businesses, to take care of their own property, or to refrain from hurting others. You know this all too well, don't you? You're no fool. You're no dreamy, unrealistic optimist. You know just how nasty Americans can be to one another.

You might be accused of being a cynic, but at least you're a realistic cynic. That's why you are a bureaucrat. That's why you are committing yourself to public service within a government regulatory agency. That's why you are reading this book. You know that the safety, well-being, mental and physical health, as well as the education and personal improvement of American citizens require not widespread mutual trust, but the opposite: deep civic *distrust*. Which returns us to the subject of regulations.

As a bureaucrat who is now or soon will be working for the United States government, you ought to become familiar with one of the most effective tools you will have in monitoring, controlling, and punishing untrustworthy American citizens: regulations. The very idea of regulation is that those in government assume citizens are guilty before citizens have had an opportunity to do any wrong. We'll develop this concept more in the next chapter, but for now we need only emphasize that regulations make it more difficult for sneaky Americans to do bad or irresponsible things, which is good for everyone.

To quote again from Jefferson:

> Sometimes it is said that man cannot be trusted with the government of himself. Can he then be trusted with the government of others? Or have we found angels, in the form

of kings, to govern him? Let history answer
this question.

The answer to Jefferson's question is, of course, *no*, we
have not found angels in the form of kings to govern
men and women. Jefferson and many other Founders
went on to conclude that no one in government—neither
unelected kings nor democratically elected representatives—should possess tremendous government power
over others because anyone in government, whether a
king or a representative, is likely to abuse that power and
harm the very people whom they are supposed to protect.

That was then. This is now. What Jefferson and the
other Founders did not know is that there is a solution to
the problem of those in government having too much
power and possibly abusing it. The solution is not to
restrain, restrict, limit, or direct the power of those in
government. The solution certainly has nothing to do
with the Constitution. The solution, rather, is a modern
invention of social science that substitutes rule by royal
decrees with rule by regulatory decrees and gets us much
closer to government by angels: *government by unelected,
bureaucratic regulators.*

Bureaucracy, connected directly to the power of
regulation, was invented and first marketed to the American people more than a hundred years ago as the rule of
"expertise." Social scientists sometimes refer to bureaus
of unelected government experts as the "rational state"
because those bureaus represent the rule of highly

educated, public-spirited, progressive experts. The "rational state," or the bureaucracy, is the *rule of intelligence* because it provides for stupid citizens to be ruled by intelligent bureaucratic experts.

Democratic, or popularly elected, constitutional government, by contrast, is the *rule of ignorance*. Democratic self-government has to be the rule of ignorance for the simple reason that mobs of voting citizens, who are neither bright nor sophisticated, tend to be moved more by flattery, fleeting passions, and demagoguery, than by reason, intelligence, or science.

Which do you want? Which does anyone want? The rule of intelligence or the rule of ignorance? The rule of expert bureaucrats or the rule of irrational voters and the flaky, bloviating, dim-witted popular politicians they elect?

Bureaucrats are indeed experts. They know how human beings should live because that's what they study. It's good to be told by experts what to do. Everyone wants medical advice from a physician, right? Everyone wants legal advice from a lawyer, and scientific advice from scientists. That's what bureaucracy does: It puts those who are smartest in charge and equips them with the power of making regulations to ensure that people live in ways that are best for them as determined by the smart bureaucrats in charge. Think of bureaucracy as a society of people whose lives are commanded by the latest findings of science. Think of regulations as those commands. Think of the regulatory-bureaucratic state as a brave new world where popular slogans and popular politicians have been replaced by experts with lab coats and fancy degrees. And machine guns.

That is why you must be among the most intelligent, the most insightful, the most rigorously trained of Americans. Why else would you devote yourself to a lifelong career of telling other citizens how to live, how to run their businesses, and how to raise their children—all backed by the power of government—unless you actually knew better than they how to do all those things?

Let's be candidly truthful for a moment. As a bureaucrat:

- You're smart. And the vast majority of your fellow citizens are not.
- You're trustworthy. And the vast majority of your fellow citizens are not.
- You're morally decent. And the vast majority of your fellow citizens are not.

The whole premise of modern, regulatory, bureaucratic government in the United States is the settled, scientific knowledge that Americans are too nefarious, or too stupid, or both, to govern their own lives. That's why the hallmarks of modern, progressive bureaucratic societies are:

- increased government regulation of the economy and civic life

- the substitution of bureaucratic fiat for the rule of law
- the centralization and expansion of administrative power, and the growth in government spending that accompanies it
- increasingly diminished spheres of individual liberty so that citizens can be monitored by bureaucratic regulators.

All of this, and nothing less, is required for a large, sprawling, highly complex, technologically advanced modern society of people who have proven inept at taking care of themselves and others, and who therefore cannot be trusted.

REGULATIONS: EMPOWERING YOUR DISTRUST AND SUSPICION

Modern, regulatory bureaucracy is more than mere scientific expertise. Government by bureaucracy also has a deeply moral component: Bureaucratic enforcement of regulations springs from deep distrust of morally untrustworthy citizens.

If you are keenly suspicious of how Americans might be plotting or planning to hurt others, or take advantage of others, or build structures not up to code, or drive their ATVs on trails not approved by certified government forest rangers, or sell poison labeled as medicine, or jack up the prices of certain goods so high that no one can actually buy them, then you likely have the mettle to be a lifelong bureaucrat wielding the power of regulations. Regulations equal distrust. The source of all regulations is a feeling of suspicion by some citizens towards other.

Americans need regulations and bureaucrats to enforce them because Americans are so untrustworthy. That's why Americans owe a great thanks to you. You possess exactly the right attitude and aptitude as you are about to launch your career in public service by working in a government regulatory office. You're not naïve. You don't trust others. You don't believe others. You're never going to be in a position of vulnerability where others can hurt you.

Rather, you are distrustful toward and suspicious of others. And you are about to have your distrust and suspicion empowered in ways of which you've only before dreamt: You're going to be able to enforce regulations with the full power of government behind you. And as you do that good work, your realistic cynicism will make the United States a better place, and your distrusting, regulatory control over Americans will make them better citizens and better people.

CHAPTER 2

REGULATIONS: GUILTY UNTIL PROVEN INNOCENT

E very school child knows the premise—or, at least, the alleged premise—of criminal law in the United States: *Innocent until proven guilty.*

The criminal law carries penalties that can include government taking a citizen's money in the form of a fine, government taking a citizen's liberty in the form of a prison sentence, and, in some cases, government taking a citizen's life in the form of capital punishment. In matters of criminal law, the stakes are high. That is why the burden is on government to prove beyond a reasonable doubt that a citizen is guilty of violating the law.

In a criminal case, the accused does not need to prove or demonstrate or argue *anything*. If, in the opinion of a jury, the government does not prove beyond a reasonable doubt that a defendant has violated the law, he or she is found "not guilty" and is free to go and live freely.

That does not mean the citizen is, in fact, innocent. Someone found "not-guilty" might actually be guilty of committing the crimes with which he or she was charged, and possibly guilty of other crimes, injustices, and wrongs as well. The verdict "not guilty" means merely that the government did not prove in a way satisfying to members of the jury that the accused citizen had violated the criminal law.

REGULATIONS: CLOSING LOOPHOLES IN THE CRIMINAL LAWS

But isn't that the very problem with criminal law? That whole premise of the law—innocent until proven guilty—means that many guilty people get away with their crimes, injustices, and moral wrongs simply because government prosecutors cannot prove their guilt inside a courtroom.

As a bureaucrat, however, you're smart enough to know that most people are up to no good much of the time. You know that the reality of crime is far larger than what we see in criminal courts. Criminals who get apprehended and convicted of committing one crime almost certainly have committed other crimes. And supposed non-criminals, citizens not arrested for or convicted of anything, almost certainly have committed plenty of crimes, injustices, and wrongs. They're just slippery and sneaky enough not to get caught.

In that regard, non-criminal citizens deserve more suspicion and oversight than criminals, because the non-criminals are the ones clever enough to conceal their wrong-doings and avoid the investigating eyes of law enforcement officers.

That is the very reason why bureaucrats invented regulations. That is the blind spot that regulations address, the loophole that regulations close, the problem that regulations solve. Rather than sitting back and waiting for a criminal to get caught in the act of breaking the law, regulations empower you, the bureaucrat, to monitor, control, judge, and even punish citizens before they break the law.

The whole premise of government regulations, after all, is the opposite of criminal law. The whole premise of government regulations is: *Guilty until proven innocent.* And thank goodness for that.

Here's an exercise of the imagination that helps to illuminate the purpose and design of regulations. Imagine if a day, or month, or year went by when no American citizen—not one—was caught breaking the criminal laws. Just imagine it.

Those laws would be useless. People would be hurting each other, stealing, defrauding, mislabeling foods, selling cars that explode, polluting the air, and doing all kinds of other wicked things. We know this because we know that human beings are untrustworthy creatures. Yet, in the midst of all this injustice, the laws would just sit on the shelves of libraries collecting dust, doing no good, if citizens were not caught breaking those laws, arrested, brought to trial, and punished by government.

BEING PRO-ACTIVE WITH REGULATIONS

Regulations, however, empower you, the bureaucrat, to be pro-active and go after citizens before they break any laws, criminal or otherwise. Regulations, you see, have nothing to do with laws. In fact, and as explained in the next chapter, regulations are not laws at all. Of any kind. Regulations are grants of power to bureaucrats by bureaucrats (pay special attention here) for the purposes of monitoring and controlling what citizens do, especially how they run their businesses, and monitoring and controlling every form of property they own.

Here's another exercise. Imagine large numbers of citizens in a state of lethargy, doing nothing, thinking nothing, just sitting and breathing their last breaths, waiting to die. Inactive, motionless, unproductive citizens pose no real threat to anyone for the simple reason that they're not thinking or moving. They don't need to be watched, regulated, controlled, or punished.

But now suppose that those same citizens get up and decide to do something. Some hunt for food or plant crops. Others might build shelters. Another group might organize and open a school. Later, after people have been productive, some might ask others to invest capital in research to develop medicines and medical technology as business ventures. Productive, active people who aren't satisfied with vegetating and being idle have endless possibilities in terms of the ideas they could put into action.

These people, all active and productive, full of energy and ideas, now pose all kinds of possible threats to others. They might lie to others, or be misleading. They might overcharge for their products. They might offer jobs to those they like. Or they might offer to pay too little for those jobs to people they don't like. They're exactly the kind of people who most need to be watched, regulated, controlled, and punished. So why wait until they are caught in the act of breaking some criminal law? Why wait for one person to sue another for tort damages after one has already caused damage or harm to others?

As a bureaucrat armed with the legal power of regulations, you don't have to wait. Bureaucrats create regulations with the common-sense knowledge that all citizens, or at least most of them, do unfair, unjust, and hurtful things often. Regulations, therefore, unlike laws, do not assume that citizens are innocent until proven guilty. Regulations are written with the assumption that citizens are guilty. The burden is upon each citizen to prove his or her innocence.

COMPLIANCE

Further, regulators are not so naïve as to allow citizens to prove their innocence just once. Or twice. Or three times. The idea of regulations means that citizens must prove their innocence over and over and over, at regular intervals, without end. This is the bureaucratic process known as compliance. It's an important tool with which you, the bureaucrat, must become familiar because it will greatly assist you in monitoring and controlling the lives and property of citizens, and punishing them when you find it necessary. Or maybe just enjoyable.

Compliance is the way that regulations turn the premise of criminal law on its head. Compliance means not waiting around for someone to break a law. The core idea of compliance is that everyone within the scope of a regulation is likely guilty right now, of something, or will be in the future. And everyone, within the scope of a regulation, has one, and only one, way to prove that they are innocent at the moment: by demonstrating that they are in compliance with the regulation.

Should citizens fail to demonstrate that they are in compliance, then, by definition they're *not* in compliance. They're *out* of compliance. Which means they're almost certainly hurting, stealing from, or defrauding fellow citizens in some way. Not being in compliance is synonymous with violating the rights of others. That is why bureaucrats can and should punish citizens in a host of ways, including fines and jail time, simply for failing to prove their innocence by not demonstrating that they are in compliance with regulations.

FINES: KICK 'EM WHILE THEY'RE DOWN

As a bureaucrat, never forget about the power of fines connected to regulations. Fines are one of the most effective tools you have to show greedy business owners that bureaucrats are the ones really in charge.

When a business is struggling, an owner will often make desperate attempts to save her business. She looks for ways to cut costs. She cuts corners. She starts to make bad business decisions, sometimes deliberately and other times not, as she panics about the future of her business.

Frequently, this is the beginning of a downward spiral. As a business struggles, the owner and employees fail to make customers happy, which leads to fewer customers, loss of market share, and less revenue, and the challenges for the business become even greater. Market forces in the world of business are relentless. They never stop. They never pause. A business either tops its competitors, satisfies existing customers by delivering value to them, attracts new ones, and grows, or the opposite. When the opposite happens, when a business is losing customers, a business owner will either make course corrections and improve how she runs her business, or she will soon be out of business.

In the turbulent, trying, stressful times of business failure, an owner might rip off some customers, deliver products or services inferior to what she promised, or treat her employees poorly. She might fudge the books with fake numbers. She might steal. She might do something wrong, in other words. When bad things are happening within a business, why wait for customers, employees, or others to sue the business owner? Why wait for the slow processes of criminal and tort laws, whether they apply or not? Why wait for a failing business owner to improve her business model as her competitors up their game and offer better products and services?

As a bureaucratic regulator, you can come along and slap a hefty fine on the business owner for being out of compliance or violating any of the regulations in your quiver. She need only fail to fill out a bureaucratic form correctly or any other minor transgression. It really doesn't matter. She won't have the resources to fight you legally. She's holding onto a losing business venture, while you are backed by all the resources of government. The private business owner is in no position to challenge your bureaucratic actions, including the fines you levy against her.

At the very moment a business is gasping for its last breath, you can put that business out of its misery by killing it. Just when cash reserves have been drained and a business owner is scrambling to find additional capital in order to keep the doors open, keep employees paid, and keep inventory on hand—just when a desperate business owner is almost certainly doing something wrong, whether you have evidence of wrongdoing or not—you have the power to shut down her business forever by leveling fines she cannot possibly pay.

Your fines won't actually help the business, of course. Your fines will finish it off, most likely. Your fines won't teach a business owner anything she didn't learn already from market forces and competition. Your fines also won't help the employees who are now out of a job, or the customers who now have fewer businesses from which to choose.

Fines don't actually improve the quality of business products or services because the businesses that are big enough to survive government fines simply add them to their budgets as part of their operating costs while they charge customers more in order to pay the fines. In fact, many businesses, such as big crony banking corporations and others, are able to deduct government fines from their profit statements and thereby reduce their taxable incomes. That's right: big corporations use fines to reduce their tax bill.

All of that is okay because when you levy fines against businesses, most of that money (if the fine gets paid) goes either to the United States Treasury or to various state governments. In other words, fines against businesses mean more money for bureaucrats, like you. That's an important incentive you have to fine businesses. The more fines against businesses, the more money in government coffers to hire bureaucrats and give them raises.

Most importantly, the fines levied by you will send a powerful and unmistakable message to all business owners: You, the bureaucrat, are the one calling the shots. You are in charge. You decide whether and when to levy fines, against whom, and how much those fines will be, because you have the discretion of deciding when to enforce regulations, which regulations to enforce, and against whom. The arbitrariness of how you enforce regulations and when you levy fines is a source of terrifying power over business owners. It's the power to decide whether a business remains open and tries to succeed, or is shut down. It's *your* power, as a bureaucrat. Protect it. And exercise it wisely in ways that increase your power over others.

MORE IS BETTER THAN FEWER

It's important that you understand why it's critical that there are many regulations, mountains of them, that apply one way or another, and preferably in many ways, to all citizens. If there are only a few regulations, then there will be many citizens to whom the regulations do not apply. And if many citizens operate outside the scope of regulations, then you, the bureaucrat, cannot monitor, control, and punish them. That would be social chaos. As every intelligent person knows.

It is essential to create many regulations that apply to everyone so that no citizen slips through the regulatory net.

Further, if bureaucrats are to create reams of regulations that apply to all citizens, then that requires large numbers of bureaucrats to write, catalog, and enforce regulations, and punish those who are non-compliant. That's good news for you because it means job security (as if civil service tenure wasn't enough).

DON'T REGULATE THE REGULATORS

It goes without saying, at least among educated and intelligent people, that while regulations assume citizens are guilty until they prove their innocence, and require citizens to prove their innocence repeatedly, endlessly, and in the face of ever-changing and often-unclear regulatory requirements, and while they should be voluminous and comprehensive so that they apply to everyone in multiple ways and guarantee a lifetime of work for each bureaucrat, regulations should not apply to regulators and other bureaucrats.

Those like you who devote yourselves to public service as bureaucrats have already demonstrated that you are not among the ordinary people who are likely hurting, stealing from, or defrauding someone. So, of course, bureaucrats like you are and should remain largely exempt from the regulations you enforce on others. There is simply no need for the high caliber of people working in bureaucracies to prove their innocence by complying with regulations.

Besides, imagine how expensive and inconvenient and time-consuming it'd be if government regulators and bureaucrats had to demonstrate continuously that they were in compliance with the regulations they are enforcing on others. They'd be so busy complying with regulations that they wouldn't be very productive. If regulations applied to bureaucratic regulators, they'd likely have little time to enforce regulations on the rest of the citizenry, which would be regulatory self-defeat. It'd be a remedy worse than the disease it was meant to cure.

CHAPTER 3

NON-LEGISLATORS LEGISLATING: HOW REGULATIONS ARE MADE

T o help you see clearly how regulations differ from law, let's once again take a little detour and recall how Constitutional laws used to be made, what their purpose was, and how they differ from modern regulations.

Every American who remembers the *School House Rock* videos from the 1970s knows how a bill becomes a law, at least at the federal level. That catchy tune is impossible to forget: "I'm just a bill, and I'm sittin' here on Capitol Hill…"

A bill—which originates as an idea or a proposal in the mind of some august Representative or Senator (or a crony business friend looking for a special government-sponsored favor over his competitors, or a group of envious citizens who want to punish those who have been more productive and successful than they)—must receive a majority vote in the United States House of Representatives, a majority vote in the United States Senate, and then (typically) be signed by the President of the United States, in order to become law.

There were reasons for this old system of making laws, a system that might best be described as old-fashioned and outdated Constitutional government. The framers of the United States Constitution and earlier generations of American citizens used to think it was important for *elected* members of government, who represent voting citizens, to make laws. The idea back then was that elected government servants are account-able to the American people, or at least those who voted for them, which meant that voting citizens were an important check on what kinds of laws elected members of government might pass and what kinds of power they might attempt to exercise.

The old assumption was that most elected legislators, and Presidents too, would not authorize wildly unpopular laws, or un-Constitutional laws, or laws that were bad or hurtful for the American people, because those same American people would vote the politicians out of office at the next election—or impeach them immediately, if the breach of public trust was sufficiently egregious.

DON'T EXPECT INTELLIGENCE FROM THE IGNORANT

This was a pretty good argument, as far as it went. But it didn't go very far. The much more serious problem with American law is not whether lawmakers are accountable to the people or not, but whether the laws are intelligent, wise, and informed by the latest scientific research. After all, if a modern, complex nation of sophisticated people is going to make progress, its laws (or rules or regulations) must be designed by the most intelligent scientific people who understand the way technology is changing and the ways technology changes our culture and society and the way we live.

Given this more important priority—ensuring that laws (or rules or regulations) are designed by the most intelligent scientific minds—does anyone really think that a Constitution written in 1787 can possibly provide a framework of public policy for the United States today?

If we agree that laws (or rules or regulations) should be designed by the most intelligent and best scientific minds among us, then here's the rub: The most intelligent and best scientific minds among us are usually not the kinds of people who get elected to Congress or to the Presidency.

Just ask yourself: What types of people typically get elected to government offices as Representatives, Senators, or President? Answer: The kinds of people who are most popular. Those who are good at flattering others. Those who might slip bribes to this group or make promises they cannot keep to another group. Those who fuel envy or anger in one group by mocking or denouncing those in another group.

The point is that getting elected to some government office is no guarantee of intelligence or any other virtue.

Getting elected certainly has nothing to do with scientific acumen. Getting elected is simply a popularity contest.

Here's more truth. The masses of American citizens, as a group, are not very intelligent. Oh, there might be a smart citizen here or there, sure. But overall, when acting together and numbering in the thousands or millions, Americans are not an intelligent *group*. On the contrary, a large group of Americans tends to be a fairly ignorant group. And within ignorant masses of citizens, who tends to be the most popular? The person to whom the ignorant masses can easily relate. One of their own, in other words. Yes, popular people who get elected to government positions tend to be ignorant. That's why many other ignorant people cast votes for them—because the ignorant masses see the electable politician as *one of them.*

This is why, as mentioned above in Chapter 1, what democratic, or republican, or elected constitutional government of any kind is really about is *the rule of ignorance.* That's right. Popular government by any name means the ignorant many electing the most popular among them to positions in the government. Then those ignorant few make laws for the ignorant many. It's a terrible way to govern.

REGULATIONS: SOLVING THE PROBLEM OF POPULAR LAWMAKERS

Before you throw up your hands and give in to political despair because elected self-government seems doomed to failure, stay focused. There's a solution to this problem. And the solution is something that you, the bureaucrat, already know well: regulations.

With a simple and subtle shift away from laws in the ordinary constitutional sense, a shift toward regulations, you and many other bureaucrats and regulators are moving the United States away from the rule of ignorance and in the direction of the rule of intelligence.

Several key features of regulations, in addition to those discussed above, make clear why they are superior to constitutional laws, why they are synonymous with progress, fairness, and social justice, and why they are indispensable for your future work as a bureaucrat.

FIRST, regulations are written by bureaucrats who work within regulatory agencies. Bureaucrats are not elected. They're hired based on their intelligence and expertise. Regulations, therefore, reflect the intelligence and expertise of the bureaucrats who make them, rather than reflecting the ignorance and power-hungry ambitions of elected, popular politicians.

SECOND, as bureaucrats are not elected, they're also not accountable to voters. Well, they sort of are, but only very indirectly—we'll address that subject in a later chapter. The important thing to note here is that the scientific intelligence and intellectual brilliance of bureaucrats does not get derailed by the demands of getting elected. When you become a cutting-edge, highly trained bureaucrat, the good news is that the ignorant masses of voting Americans don't need to understand what you're doing (which they're too stupid to do) because they won't be electing you.

Think about it. What do the masses of American people know about particulate emissions from a factory smokestack? What do the masses know about approving car seat belts that others designed or which medicines they should be allowed to try for themselves? What do they know about what their own kids should be learning in school or the postmodern theories of the inter-dynamics of race studies, gender identities, and economic class oppression that form the policies that government uses to tell business owners how to run their businesses and treat their employees? Answer: The masses know little or nothing about these and many other subjects.

So why would anyone want the ignorant masses voting on who should or should not work at the Environmental Protection Agency or the Department of Transportation or the Food and Drug Administration or the Department of Education or the Department of Labor or the Equal Employment Opportunity Commission? Further, why would anyone want regulators and bureaucrats trying to explain regulations to the ignorant voting public, when the ignorant voting public can never in a million years understand regulatory technicalities?

It's best that bureaucrats and regulators are un-elected. This ensures that regulations continue to be intelligent, rational, and backed by scientific evidence, precisely because they are not subject to the interference of ignorant voting masses of citizens.

THIRD, the Congress of the United States is one of the least efficient organizations ever designed by human minds. Elected lawmakers represent so many different and opposing constituents that it becomes nearly impossible to get anything done in Congress. One Representative demands that Congress follow the Constitution, then some Senator demands that the Constitution be ignored, then a President comes along who doesn't know what the Constitution means because he or she never read it. Round and round they go, all representing different interests, bogged down in gridlock, with endless debates and discussions and airing of different opinions and points of view. The result is that we go in circles and make no progress forward.

But you, the bureaucrat, will be working inside a government agency that has the power to issue regulations. And since regulations are not laws—they don't require a vote by the House or the Senate, or any approval from the President—you, along with your bureaucratic colleagues, can figure out what policies are best for the American people, how best they should live their lives and run their businesses. In an instant you can enshrine your insights and advice into a regulation that has the full power of law.

Further, you and your fellow bureaucrats can crank out lots of regulations in very short order, far more regulations than the laws passed by Congress, for example. Below are two charts provided by the Regulatory Studies Center within the Columbian College of Arts and Sciences at the George Washington University in Washington, D.C.

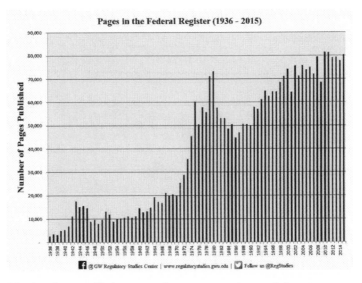

Notice how efficient regulatory agencies and bureaucrats have become at churning out regulations. They now add, on average, around 80,000 pages of regulations in the

Federal Register and almost 180,000 pages in the *United States Code of Federal Regulations*—per year.

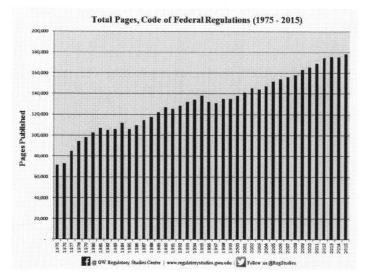

These graphs reveal much, but they hide the most insidious truth about regulations: They're not laws. Regulations are not designed, written, or approved by elected legislators. No President signs them. Yet, in and out of courtrooms, regulations have the full power of law. Citizens must obey regulations, or suffer consequences, which can include fines and imprisonment. You, the bureaucrat, can control others and command how they live, backed up by the full force of government, without ever getting elected or requiring the consent of your fellow citizens. And you can create more regulations than anyone can possibly know or keep track of, which means you always have the upper hand.

CHAPTER 4

NON-EXECUTIVES ENFORCING AND NON-JUDGES JUDGING: HOW REGULATIONS COME TO HAVE THE POWER OF LAW

L et's again use the Constitutionalism of the American Founding, as a contrast, to help illuminate how different and radical modern regulations are.

In *The Federalist Papers* and other literature from the American Founding, the Founders emphasized the importance of the "separation of powers" as an important way to mitigate the danger of tyranny. In *Federalist* #47, for example, James Madison wrote: "The accumulation of all powers—legislative, executive, and judicial—in the same hands, whether of one, a few, or many, and whether hereditary, self-appointed, or elected, may justly be pronounced the very definition of tyranny." Which means the way to prevent tyranny is to prevent all political powers—legislative, executive, and judicial—from being exercised by the same hands.

The problem, as the Founders saw it, begins with the simple observation that legislative power is the power to make laws. Executive power is the power to execute or enforce laws. Judicial power is the power to judge whether someone has broken or violated the government's laws. When one person or one group of people in government exercises all three political powers, there is virtually no check on the use or abuse of government power. That's why Madison described all three powers being vested in one set of hands as "the very definition of tyranny."

From this definition of tyranny, the Founders designed the Constitution in a way that enshrined the separation of powers into the structure of government. Members of the three branches were selected in different ways, served for differing amounts of time, and were accountable to different constituencies. Representatives were elected directly by the voting citizens in diverse Congressional districts. Senators were, under the original Constitution, chosen by state legislators. The President was to be selected through an Electoral College that gave influence to states over a simple national popular vote. Justices on the Supreme Court were not elected at all, but rather nominated by a President and confirmed by the Senate.

The framers of the Constitution relied little on expectations that elected servants would be men or women of especially good character or virtue. They relied much on the structure of government, which included the separation of powers. Each branch of government possessed certain checks and powers that could be used to rein in the other branches. And being accountable to different constituencies made each branch less likely to tolerate abuses of power or exercises of un-Constitutional power by the other branches.

That's why, under the Constitution, only the legislative branch (Congress) had power to pass laws, only the executive branch (President) had power to enforce laws, and only the judicial branch (Supreme Court) had power to judge when there was a question of whether someone had violated the laws.

SEPARATION OF POWERS: *SOOO* INEFFICIENT

The problem with the entire separation of powers principle is that it makes controlling citizens and confiscating their property so inefficient. There's almost always gridlock of some kind between the legislative and executive branches, grinding the legislative process to a virtual halt.

Further, the judicial branch is often asked to interpret laws and policies that it did not participate in designing, so it usually doesn't know with certainty what those laws and policies were intended to mean. And when the judicial branch gets around to rendering a decision, it lacks any power to enforce it. In the famous 1954 case of *Brown v. Board of Education*, for example, the Supreme Court struck down racial segregation in public schools. A full decade after the Court had issued its opinion, however, public schools remained racially segregated across the United States. Why? Because the judicial branch had no power to enforce its rulings.

The real results of incorporating separation of powers into the constitutional design of a government are inefficiency, ineffectiveness, delays, and government impotence. The American Founders simply did not understand this. They were wrong.

Regardless of the original Constitution and the Founders' attempt to separate political powers and keep them separated, you might be wondering if it's possible to combine all three powers of government into one governmental body. Here's the good news: It *is*. There is a way to combine the legislative, executive, and judicial powers into one set of government hands. That's precisely what modern regulatory agencies do. And that is why regulatory agencies are much more efficient, much more modern, and much more progressive forms of government than the old, tired Constitutional separation of powers.

Here's how it works, at least at the federal level. Typically, Congress passes a law that creates a bureaucratic-regulatory agency. These laws rarely include language that makes clear what citizens are required to do or are prohibited from doing. Rather, these laws begin by identifying a problem—it could be unfair labor practices, or dirty air and water, or unsafe toys for children, or any other problem, real or imagined—and then create and authorize a regulatory agency to solve the problem. Regulatory laws passed by Congress vest an agency with the power to make regulations that the bureaucratic regulators believe will solve the problem.

It doesn't really matter whether the regulations issued by the agency ever actually solve the identified problem, or any other problems. And it makes no sense for citizens to read the laws, because the laws don't specify what is or is not prohibited (or mandated). What matters is that the regulators and bureaucrats inside the government agency, which includes you, write regulations based on their expertise. Regulations can be and might be designed to solve the problem identified by Congress in the original statutory law. Or, bureaucrats can design regulations for other goals, perhaps goals of their own, not identified by Congress. It really is up to you, the bureaucrat, to decide the content and purpose of regulations.

CHEVRON DOCTRINE: EVERY BUREAUCRAT'S FRIEND

See, regulators can pursue their own purposes that might differ from the purposes originally identified by Congress in the authorizing legislation. It's okay because 1) Congress never really had any Constitutional authority to create regulatory agencies in the first place, so it's not as if anyone is going to raise Constitutional concerns when bureaucrats within an agency pursue their own agenda. And 2) the United States Supreme Court has contrived a wonderful argument, known as the "Chevron Doctrine," according to which American courts defer to regulators whenever there is a question about how much power a regulatory agency has under the laws that created it.[3]

Also, keep in mind that after creating a regulatory agency, Congress often passes subsequent, amending legislation that expands the scope and power of the agency it's already created. And many of these pieces of legislation run to hundreds or even thousands of pages long. The good news for you is that almost no one knows what's in those hundreds and thousands of pages of legislation, much less what's in the tens and hundreds of thousands of pages of regulations issued every year by regulatory agencies. So the chances of anyone objecting that a particular regulation violates a specific law are less than slim. They're microscopic. When you're in the position of being an unelected bureaucrat, you have the latitude to do almost anything you want, so long as your supervisor remains happy, an important subject addressed in Chapter 11.

After writing regulations, a regulatory agency then enforces them upon citizens through compliance re-

---

[3] For budding bureaucrats who think Democrats are your only friends in government, don't forget the Republicans. Republican-nominated Justices on the Supreme Court, especially John Paul Stevens and Antonin Scalia, are the ones who invented and later expanded the Chevron Doctrine. It's a gift Republicans gave to you bureaucrats and regulators because it has been a great aid in expanding the power and scope of the modern administrative-regulatory-bureaucratic state.

quirements, inspections, audits, and other forms of monitoring. If a question comes up about whether someone has violated a regulation, the bureaucrats convene a hearing. Usually the judge who presides over the hearing is employed by the very same regulatory agency that issued the regulation in the first place. That's right: Regulators within a government regulatory agency exercise legislative power by writing and issuing regulations that have the power of law, enforcing those regulations, and judging whether there has been a violation of the regulations or not. Are you starting to see how easily and effectively regulations displace the entire Constitutional principle of separation of powers?

In a 1994 essay from the *Harvard Law Review*, Boston University Law Professor Gary Lawson described how the Federal Trade Commission works. His account is a perfect example of how virtually all federal bureaucratic-regulatory agencies combine the powers of government in one set of hands:

> The Commission promulgates substantive rules of conduct [and regulations]. The Commission then considers whether to authorize investigations into whether the Commission's rules have been violated. If the Commission authorizes an investigation, the investigation is conducted by the Commission, which reports its findings to the Commission. If the Commission thinks that the Commission's findings warrant an enforce-

ment action, the Commission issues a complaint. The Commission's complaint that a
Commission rule has been violated is then
prosecuted by the Commission and adjudi-
cated by the Commission. The Commission
adjudication can either take place before the
full Commission or before a semi-
autonomous administrative law judge. If the
Commission chooses to adjudicate before an
administrative law judge rather than before
the Commission and the decision is adverse
to the Commission, the Commission can ap-
peal to the Commission.

This makes for an incredibly efficient way to control
citizens and dictate how they run their businesses, raise
their families, use their property, and generally live their
lives. The regulators who sit in judgment when there's an
allegation that a regulation has been violated or ignored
work with and know the regulators who enforce the
regulations, and they all work with and know the regulators who wrote and issued the regulations. So there's little
uncertainty about the meaning of the regulations in
question, and the power of any regulatory agency can
slam down upon any citizen swiftly, rather than waiting
for slow, indifferent courts to act, with their unending
"due process" procedures, or trying to get the executive
branch to enforce what the legislative branch has passed.

In rare instances, controversies between citizens and
the regulatory agencies that run their lives and businesses
end up in a courtroom with an actual, Constitutional

judge, one that works within the judicial branch of government and hears cases involving actual, Constitutionally passed laws. But, again, that is rare. And, as stated above, judges and courts are incredibly deferential to whatever regulators and bureaucrats say needs to be done in any particular situation. When there is any kind of challenge to the power and force that bureaucratic regulators have exercised, judges simply ask the bureaucratic regulators if they believe the power they, themselves, exercised was warranted and legitimate. If bureaucrats can demonstrate some rational connection—*any* connection, really—between the regulations they're enforcing and the goal they're trying to achieve, then most judges and courts will give the bureaucratic regulators a stamp of approval to carry on. That's the Chevron Doctrine.

And this is why you and the millions of your non-military, unelected, civil service bureaucratic colleagues working in government truly are an improvement to the United States way of governing. You *are* the progress of which so many speak.

REGULATORS ENFORCING REGULATIONS EXPAND BUREAUCRACIES

An added benefit to regulators enforcing their own regulations is that it expands the ranks and power of bureaucrats, which is good news for you. An example from the Department of Agriculture under President Franklin Roosevelt is telling.

Running for President in 1932, FDR promised to help farmers by getting the prices of wheat, corn, dairy, and other farm products to go up, which would be good for farmers (and kind of sucky for the poor slobs who would have to buy those goods at higher prices, a subject discussed in Chapter 7).

FDR and the New Dealers in Congress came up with the Agricultural Adjustment Act of 1933, which authorized the United States Department of Agriculture to create regulations that would require farmers to not farm up to 25% of their land in return for government subsidies. Get it? Government would pay farmers *not to farm*. The result, FDR hoped, would be immediate revenue for the farmers in the form of the subsidies, coupled with higher prices for farm produce caused by the regulated reduction in farm production, meaning lower supplies of wheat, corn, dairy, etc.

It sounded like a great plan at first. Then FDR received the first annual report from the Secretary of Agriculture. Guess what was happening? Farmers received their subsidy checks from Congress, cashed them, spent the money, then went on to plant crops on *all* their land. They were not leaving 25% barren as the regulators had commanded them to do.

What were FDR and the bureaucrats in the Department of Agriculture to do? Well, they did what any intelligent bureaucrat would do: They hired more bureaucrats to go out and inspect farm fields to make sure farmers were in compliance with federal regulations.

The next problem, FDR soon learned, was that after farmers received their subsidy checks and cashed them, and the bureaucratic government inspectors arrived, the farmers used part of the subsidies to bribe the inspectors. Given that FDR and the Department of Agriculture could not trust the farmers or the government inspectors, they opted to hire a second tier of bureaucratic inspectors who would inspect the inspectors—sort of like super-bureaucrats, or regulators of regulators. This, however, did not solve the problem. The corruption and bribery simply continued. And grew.

This led FDR and the Department of Agriculture to purchase the largest fleet of airplanes in the United States at that time, each equipped with a sophisticated camera, to fly over farms and monitor who was and was not in compliance with farming regulations. Very quickly the Department of Agriculture ballooned into one of the largest bureaucratic organizations within the federal government. Even then, problems of non-compliance, corruption, and bribery remained unsolved.

Want to know the ironic thing? Government created subsidies and regulations, and ordered inspectors to inspect other inspectors, and launched airplanes to monitor farmers from the skies, all in an effort to *reduce* farm outputs and thereby *raise* the prices of corn, wheat, and dairy, and all to make farmers happy so they'd vote again for FDR and his Democratic friends in Congress. Yet, at the same time, profit-seeking business owners improved fertilizers, seed, and farming technologies. Farming became more efficient, more productive. The result was that even farmers planting only 75% of their land began to produce more than when they were planting 100% of their land. As early as 1935, production rates of some crops were actually higher than they had been before all the government programs and regulatory restrictions began.

The actual results of these government programs and regulations, however, don't matter, as we'll discuss in Chapter 6. The important lesson here is that one important function of government regulations and bureaucracies is to create more regulations and more bureaucracy. Which is great job security for you. As bureaucrats write, enforce, and judge more regulations, the nation will require more regulations and more bureaucrats. It's a win-win process for unelected government employees.

Another important function of regulations and bureaucracies is that the more regulations are issued, and the more bureaucracies are created to enforce them, the more the regulatory-bureaucratic state becomes what some social scientists call the "permanent government." As the permanent government grows, elections come to be increasingly unimportant for bureaucrats. If you're a bureaucrat at a federal regulatory agency, already in command of citizens and their property, what does it really matter to you who wins this or that election? It doesn't. It doesn't matter whether a Democrat or Republican becomes the next President. It doesn't matter which political party controls Congress. After all, members of Congress and Presidents don't issue or enforce regulations, *you* do.

The permanent government of the modern bureaucratic state displaces the government authorized by citizens through elections. This can be seen by the fact that when citizens have a problem with some bureaucratic-regulatory government agency, and an election is approaching, those citizens don't actually know how voting for or against any particular candidate will influence the bureaucratic-regulatory government agency with which they have a problem.

Yet—and here's the real beauty of it—Americans continue to focus all their political attention and energy on elections. And partisan politics. They actually care, deeply, who gets elected to various government offices and who does not. As a bureaucrat, you want Americans to continue focusing on elections and squawking at each other over partisan differences. You want Democrats and Republicans to continue mocking and making fun of each other, yelling at each other, because electoral politics is the single best diversion that keeps the attention of citizens, voters, and taxpayers away from growing bureaucracies and your growing power base in the permanent government.

This points to an important political lesson for bureaucrats that's rarely discussed in classrooms or textbooks: how law can serve to distract voting citizens, politically, from bureaucrats working deep inside the permanent government.

When law serves its old-fashioned, classically liberal purpose—offering equal protection for the person and property of each citizen, nothing more—domestic politics become peaceful, even boring. When law operates in a negative sense, merely prohibiting or punishing those who violate the individual rights of others, political questions about who should be elected to occupy which government office become less important, less urgent. Politics are not all-consuming and emotionally exhausting when the law gives no advantages to some citizens at the expense of others.

This is dangerous for you because if citizens are not distracted by politics, they might start focusing on the work, the results, and the budgets of bureaucrats. You do not want public attention, much less scrutiny. You want the public to remain distracted as much as possible.

When law is designed as an instrument to take from some people what they produced or earned and give it to others, however, politics become the most pressing matter of the day. Every day. Politics become turbulent, divisive, even vicious and sometimes violent.

When law is used to transfer wealth from some to others, everyone wants to be beneficiaries. No one wants to pay. And no one can simply ignore the politics of wealth transfer because every person will become either a beneficiary or a payer, either a recipient or a provider, depending on how the law is written, executed, and judged. The way to make sure one is a beneficiary instead of a payer is to control the legal transfer of wealth, control who makes the law, how it gets enforced, and who will sit in judgment of the law when controversies arise. Control requires power. In a democratic society like the United States, power comes from a majority coalition of voters. That is why politics become turbulent, divisive, vicious, and sometimes violent—a desperate power struggle to be the majority—when law is used to take from some people what they produced and earned and give it to others.

This is good for you because the more citizens are distracted by turbulent, divisive, all-consuming, and emotionally exhausting politics, the less likely they are to pay attention to what you and other bureaucrats are doing. It's in your interest, therefore, to use all tools at your disposal, including the powers of the government agency in which you work, to advocate for laws and public policies that confiscate wealth from some citizens and transfer it to others. It's also in your interest to use all the tools and powers available to you to intimidate, harass, or squash anyone and any organizations promoting old-fashioned law limited to protecting the person and property of each citizen.

CHAPTER 5

DON'T WORRY ABOUT THE CONSTITUTION: YOU HAVE IMPORTANT WORK TO DO

After the discussion in the previous chapter regarding the separation of powers and the Constitution, some of you might be wondering right about now, perhaps even worrying, whether regulatory agencies and the many positions of bureaucratic power within them are Constitutional.

The short answer is that you are a bureaucrat and you have no time for such frivolous questions.

The longer answer is no, regulatory agencies and the many positions of bureaucratic power within them are not Constitutional. But only if one reads the Constitution in the most pinched way possible, paying attention to the actual words of the Constitution, what they meant at the time they were written, and the ensuing discussions of the day about the Constitution's meaning. Fortunately for you, only a few extremists and conservative critics of bureaucracy read the Constitution that way.

To judge modern regulatory agencies against the standards of the Constitution makes little sense. It's an odd thing to do. It's anachronistic. Today's regulatory agencies were designed by modern, progressive public policy experts and academic social scientists, whereas the Constitution was written by amateurs who were racist, sexist, homophobic, greedy, and deeply immoral. Regulatory agencies are created by modern professionals and progressive politicians who promise that they care about children, poor people, transgendered people, and the environment. The Constitution is old, outdated, not at all green, and utterly irrelevant to our lives as 21st century Americans. There was no Internet when the Constitution was written, after all, so what does it matter whether regulations, the agencies that issue them, and the bureaucrats who enforce them align with the Constitution or not?

Still, there are conservative activists and extremists who will try to use Constitutional arguments and principles to limit your power as a bureaucrat. It's good for you to understand what they might say, either in a courtroom or in the court of public opinion, so that you can be prepared to respond with the appropriate counterarguments or ridicule. What follows is a summary of the Constitutional case against modern, unelected regulatory agencies.

THE CONSTITUTION

Article I, Section 1 of the United States Constitution, the very first sentence after the famous Preamble, states: "All legislative powers herein granted shall be vested in a Congress of the United States, which shall consist of a Senate and House of Representatives."

1. So what legislative powers does Congress possess, according to the Constitution? Does Congress possess all imaginable legislative powers? Do members of Congress possess any and all powers to do whatever they think is good, or fair, or right? Um, no. Congress possesses the legislative powers "herein granted"—meaning the powers granted to Congress herein the Constitution—and no more. The very clause that vests legislative power in the Congress also limits legislative power by making clear that Congress possesses only the powers "herein granted" and no other powers.

2. Read through the list of powers granted to Congress in the Constitution. It might shock you how short that list is. (Hint: There's no power to regulate health insurance or education, or to confiscate wealth from some people and transfer it to others, or to fund local police departments or local schools, among many thousands of other things *not* in there.)

3. Article I, Section 1 of the Constitution does not say that some legislative powers will be vested in a Congress, while other legislative powers will be

vested in an EPA, and DOE, and DOL, and HHS, and OSHA, and IRS, and EEOC, and CSPC, and SEC, and FDIC, and FRB, etc.

4. The Constitution provides a short list of powers that Congress possesses. Nowhere does the Constitution grant to Congress the power to *delegate* its legislative power to independent regulatory agencies such as the EPA, and DOE, and DOL, and HHS, and OSHA, and IRS, and EEOC, and CSPC, and SEC, and FDIC, and FRB, etc.

Now, let's get real, and serious. As a bureaucrat, you want to know whether anyone knows or cares about these old-fashioned Constitutional interpretations. Thankfully, most elected politicians don't. Most members of Congress and Presidents have little interest in the Constitution, if they've even read it. Most Justices on the Supreme Court neither know nor care about the Constitution, except to the degree they occasionally need new meanings of old Constitutional words in order to justify new government programs. And even then, they usually rely on the Constitutional sophistries conjured by law school professors and other academics. Bureaucrats and regulators certainly don't pay any attention to the Constitution. If they cared about old-fashioned Constitutional principles, they'd be unable to do the great amounts of good they do for the public. And that's what matters.

Further, ignoring much or all of the Constitution is no new thing. Academic social scientists, who teach in the colleges and universities of the United States, have been explaining to others for more than a century why the United States Constitution is not only irrelevant, but positively gets in the way. In his first published book, for example, Woodrow Wilson, who was the first President of the United States to hold a Ph.D. and who had a long and distinguished career as an academician, compared the Constitution to "political witchcraft." Why? Because the Constitution keeps the United States government frozen back in the time it was written, 1787.

As Wilson remarked, "The makers of the Constitution constructed the federal government upon a theory of checks and balances which was meant to limit the operation of each part and allow to no single part or organ of it a dominating force." He continued:

> The government of the United States was constructed upon the Whig theory of political dynamics, which was a sort of unconscious copy of the Newtonian theory of the universe...Some single law, like the law of gravitation, swung each system of thought and gave it its principle of unity. Every sun, every planet, every free body in the spaces of the heavens, the world itself, is kept in its place and reined to its course by the attraction of bodies that swing with equal order and precision about it, themselves governed

by the nice poise and balance of forces which
give the whole system of the universe its
symmetry and perfect adjustment.

The problem, Wilson explained, is that "no government
can be successfully conducted upon so mechanical a
theory." Government, after all, is not a machine. It is a
living, organic thing that must grow, develop, and adjust
to changing circumstances, technologies, and cultural
views about what is right and wrong, what should be
lawful, and what should not. "In our own day," Wilson
wrote, "whenever we discuss the structure or development of anything, whether in nature or in society, we
follow Mr. Darwin, but before Mr. Darwin, the Founders
followed Newton."

The fact is any government, and any constitution,
will fail to serve the people if they demand that a constitution be understood forever as it was originally written.
Constitutional or legal originalism is a death sentence for
any nation. Original intent is national suicide. Why?
Because, as Wilson summed up correctly, "Living political
constitutions must be Darwinian in structure and in
practice."

We don't live in 1787. The world is different than it
was in 1787. The United States, in particular, is a different
place. We've evolved in many ways. Even human nature
is different—we today are better than, smarter than, and
morally superior to people in the past. New forms of
technology, gigantic cities, the rise of sprawling multi-

national corporations, the production, creation, and concentration of unprecedented amounts of wealth, mass communications, mass production of foods and medicines, modern transportation, and universal schooling for everyone…the American Founders could never have conceived of any of it. It's irrational to allow all that activity, growth, and evolutionary development to continue without bureaucratic supervision and regulatory control.

After all, what do scientists, engineers, and other kinds of entrepreneurial innovators know about the technologies and products they're inventing or improving? Not nearly as much as the regulators who tell them what they may and may not do.

If we modern Americans bind ourselves by an old-fashioned interpretation of the Constitution and fail to protect citizens by failing to control their property and monitoring what they do, then the Constitution truly will prove to be "witchcraft," an instrument of social evil, just as Wilson described it.

As we've already discussed, popular politicians are not elected because of their virtue or their brains. It's unreasonable to expect elected government officials to figure out and solve the myriad problems arising in our modern, complex, technological world. They cannot. And even if they could—even if they did have brains and virtue—a few hundred members of Congress working with a President cannot tackle the countless new problems that pop up every day all across the United States and the virtual world of the Internet. Only a large, regulatory state with teams of bureaucrats can solve the endless problems of the modern world, and monitor and control citizens through ever-changing regulations, as citizens think, talk, make choices, and move from one situation to another.

Justice William Brennan was absolutely correct when he remarked in 1986 that the Constitution belongs to "a world dead and gone." The day of Constitutionalism is over. Or, at least, old-fashioned, original intent Constitutionalism. Today is the day of the bureaucrat. The government administrator. The regulator. Today is *your* day.

You have important work to do. You will guide citizens as they live their lives. You will protect them from dangers seen and unseen. You will make sure they get the best deals for their dollars and that the products they buy are safe, sound, and environmentally friendly. And you'll make sure that no one's feelings are hurt when they walk into any business, even before they buy something. You will direct citizens so that they learn and do the work that our progressive nation needs them to do. You will be their shepherd, their leader, their protector, their trainer, their teacher, their therapist, their judge, their corrections officer, their warden. Your role, as a bureaucrat, is far more important than any outdated, old-fashioned interpretation of a Constitution written before trains, phones, or computers were invented. So, please, don't give the Constitution another second of thought.

PART
II

RESULTS
OF A
BUREAUCRAT'S
WORK

CHAPTER 6

RESULTS DON'T MATTER, INTENTIONS DO

For bureaucrats, this is one of the most basic and important lessons you can learn. It will put your career as a government agent in proper perspective. It doesn't matter if your efforts are successful or not. It doesn't matter if your work is effective at accomplishing goals set by you or others. *Results don't matter.* What matters—the only thing that matters, really—are your intentions.

This is not mere opinion or conjecture. This is fact. As a bureaucrat, you will be judged by elected politicians who control the budget of the department or agency where you work. And you will be judged by fellow bureaucrats, pundits, and political commentators. You might also be judged by the American public. But you will never, ever, be judged on your professional performance or on whether you achieved any particular goals. You won't be judged on whether you actually did any good. You will be judged by your intentions. So make sure your intentions are good. Or, at a minimum, say out loud and in public that your intentions are good. Often.

EDUCATION

If you doubt this, consider, as merely one example—but a significant one—the United States Department of Education. Created in 1979, one of its original goals, according to the statutory language and executive order that created it, was "to strengthen the Federal commitment to ensuring access to equal educational opportunity for every individual."

Today, that Department employs approximately 5000 well-paid bureaucrats, almost all of whom teach no students whatsoever. The average salary in the DOE is about $105,000 and some salaries climb far above $150,000, not to mention the host of benefits that come with any federal government job. If we take a conservative estimate of $105,000 as an average cost to the taxpayer for each bureaucrat at the Department, and we multiply that number by the 5000 employees who work there, we learn that the government takes roughly $525 million per year from taxpayers to spend on salaries for bureaucrats at the DOE. In 2015, the total budget for the Federal Department of Education was a whopping $87 billion.

Yet all that money spent on and by all those bureaucrats does not equate to ensuring access to equal educational opportunity for every individual. "Access" to "educational opportunities" is in no way "equal" today for every American child. Some children have parents who provide learning opportunities that other children never experience. Yet that's okay. The DOE continues to grow, its budget continues to get bigger, and the bureaucrats it employs continue to get pay raises. Achieving a goal simply doesn't matter. See?

Another key objective of the Department, according to its own internal documents, is "to promote improvements in the quality and usefulness of education."

Since 1979, federal spending on K-12 education, channeled through the DOE to states, counties, and school districts, has skyrocketed. The United States government spends more taxpayer dollars on education, in total and per pupil, than ever before. Vastly more. And

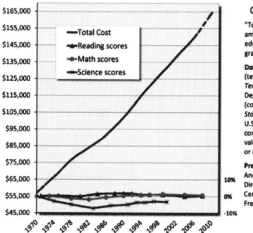

Trends in inflation-adjusted cost of a complete K-12 public education ($ scale), and achievement of 17-Year-Olds (% scale)

Legend:
- Total Cost
- Reading scores
- Math scores
- Science scores

Y-axis ($ scale): $45,000 to $165,000
X-axis years: 1970, 1974, 1978, 1982, 1986, 1990, 1994, 1998, 2002, 2006, 2010
Secondary scale: 10%, 0%, -10%

Cato Institute

"Total cost" is the whole amount spent on the K-12 education of a student graduating in the given year.

Data sources
(test scores): NAEP, *Long Term Trends* reports, U.S. Department of Education (cost): *Digest of Education Statistics 2011*, Table 191, U.S. DOE, CPI adjusted to constant 2012 $. Missing values linearly interpolated or extrapolated.

Prepared Sept. 2012 by: Andrew J. Coulson, Director, Cato Institute Center for Educational Freedom

yet, as the charts here show, there's been no significant, measurable improvement in key educational indicators.

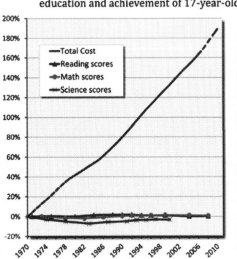

Trends in inflation-adjusted total cost of a K-through-12 public education and achievement of 17-year-olds (U.S.)

Cato Institute

"Total cost" is the whole amount spent on the K-12 education of a student graduating in the given year. We graph the percent change in that amount--and in test scores--over time.

Data sources
(test scores): NAEP, *Long Term Trends* reports, U.S. Department of Education (cost): *Digest of Education Statistics 2011*, Table 191, U.S. DOE, CPI adjusted to constant 2012 $. Missing values linearly interpolated or extrapolated.

Prepared Sept. 2012 by: Andrew J. Coulson, Director, Cato Institute Center for Educational Freedom

These charts have been prepared by the Cato Institute; however, a quick Internet search for "education spending and results" will reveal many charts and graphs and data sets, all of which tell the same basic story. In some cases, educational performance has actually gone *down* as federal funding for education has gone up.

The bottom line is that huge increases in government spending and bureaucratic power over education failed to improve education. But that doesn't matter. If you focus on the results of government programs, government regulations, and government spending for education, you are missing the whole lesson of this chapter.

What matters is: Those who actively support increases in government spending and bureaucratic power over education claim to love children and care deeply about education. What matters, in other words, are their *intentions.* If their intentions are good, then anyone who opposes increases in federal spending on education in general, or opposes expanding the role of the federal Department of Education in particular, must have bad intentions. Those opposed to more government spending on education clearly do not love children. They probably hate children. And they clearly don't care about education. They probably hate education, too.

As long as we demonize opponents of increased government spending on education, their reputations will be diminished, their credibility will evaporate, and their efforts to reduce government spending will fail—regardless of how much waste, fraud, corruption, or incompetency exists at the Department of Education. All of which is good for you because it means more job security and likely higher pay in the future.

Never lose sight of the fact that results don't matter. This has been proven many, many times by many, many other government agencies and offices and programs and policies and regulations.

The Wild Horse and Burro Program, as just another example, is part of the Federal Bureau of Land Management (BLM). The program charges BLM bureaucrats with the goal of managing, well, horses and burros. After failing to achieve that goal, the BLM Advisory Board's recommended solution was slaughtering 45,000 beautiful wild horses. This death-for-wild-horses proposal likely would have been carried out except for last-minute public outrage. Turns out Americans don't like tens of thousands of horses being destroyed (even though BLM bureaucrats routinely sell horses it cannot manage, on the cheap, to private slaughter-houses owned by ranchers with crony connections to BLM bureaucrats).

Regardless of whether those horses are actually killed or not, the mere prospect of such large-scale horse euthanasia highlights the failures of BLM bureaucrats and the Wild Horse and Burro Program. The Wild Horse and Burro Program fails to do the very thing for which it was created: to manage wild horses and burros. Those failures provide a perfect justification for the Director of the Bureau of Land Management—and the Secretary of the Interior, to whom the BLM Director reports—to demand a bigger budget from Congress for the 10,000 bureaucrats employed by the BLM. Which is exactly what they did.

It simply does not matter whether any government programs, policies, or regulations, or the bureaucrats who enforce them, achieve their published goals or not. Ever.

WAR ON DRUGS

On June 17, 1971, a high-ranking government official announced: "America's public enemy number one in the

United States is drug abuse. In order to fight and defeat this enemy, it is necessary to wage a new, all-out offensive." The government official was President Richard Nixon. His speech marked the beginning of the federal government's War on Drugs.

Working together, Republican Nixon and a Democrat-controlled Congress passed the Comprehensive Drug Abuse Prevention and Control Act, of which the Controlled Substances Act was part. They also created a new federal police agency, the Drug Enforcement Administration (DEA). They did all of this, and more, despite the fact that the Constitution grants no power for Congress or any part of the federal government to regulate drugs.

As a comparison, consider that a mere generation before the War on Drugs, when members of Congress wanted to regulate and prohibit the manufacture, sale, and transportation of alcohol, they first sought ratification of the 18th Amendment, which vested Congress with the Constitutional power needed to wage a kind of "war on alcohol." The government effort to stamp out alcoholism, known as Prohibition, was a miserable failure surrounded by rising levels of violence and organized crime—as well as rising rates of alcoholism—and soon led to the 21st Amendment, which repealed the 18th. That was before the United States had become thoroughly progressive, however. In the 1920s, citizens and their elected representatives cared about the results of government policies and programs.

Further, members of Congress back then acknowledged that they had no Constitutional power to regulate alcohol, which is why they asked the American people to expand the powers of Congress via Constitutional Amendment. The Constitution also vests no power in Congress or in the President to criminalize the possession or use of drugs. But that didn't stop Nixon and members of Congress in the 1970s, who were much more progressive than politicians had been in the 1920s. Without any Constitutional authority, they simply passed federal laws regarding drugs, a subject that's supposed to remain in the jurisdiction of state and local governments. They created federal enforcement agencies, regulatory agencies, and they started to spend other people's money. Lots of money.

Now more than four decades old, the War on Drugs has racked up costs over $1.5 trillion. It has been a great success for bureaucrats, from regulators to DEA and FBI agents to defense lawyers and prosecutors, to prison guards. In terms of "defeating drug abuse," however, which was its stated purpose, the War on Drugs has been another miserable failure. Drug use and abuse in the last four decades, including addiction to illicit drugs and the many costs associated with it, as well as national and international drug trafficking, have not only not decreased, in many cases they've increased, greatly, as some drugs have become more popular among users and dealers while other drugs have become less popular.

The big difference between the old "war on alcohol," or Prohibition, and the modern War on Drugs is that results mattered during Prohibition. In fact, lack of results and bad results eventually brought an end to Prohibition. But in our new world of progressivism, where results don't matter when it comes to government programs, regulations, and the bureaucrats who administer them, there is no end in sight for the War on Drugs.

If you're looking for more proof that results don't matter when it comes to government programs, check out how Americans actually abandoned a voluntary system of assistance for individuals in need that was quite successful, in favor of adopting a modern, centralized government welfare system whose results have been disastrous.

WELFARE

Before politicians during the New Deal-era nationalized welfare and centralized its administration in Washington, D.C., the United States had a noble tradition of providing assistance to fellow citizens in dire straits. In terms of results, it worked very well.

That tradition stretched back to the early colonial period, even before the American Revolution, and remained intact, robust, and eminently helpful for those who most needed temporary help throughout the 19th and into the early 20th century. That tradition was eclipsed in the

1930s and 1940s, and even more in the 1960s, by progressive welfare policies, introducing the kinds of modern, centralized, bureaucratic government welfare programs that we continue to see in the United States today.

Important differences distinguish the earlier forms of assistance from the modern, progressive, bureaucratic forms of welfare that emerged later. And those differences provide more evidence that when it comes to government programs and bureaucrats, results don't matter, intentions do. Here's a quick review of those differences.

LOCAL VERSUS NATIONAL

Earlier forms of assistance were local, where neighbors and fellow citizens of a community knew which families had suffered unexpected loss and truly needed temporary help versus those individuals who simply didn't want to work and were looking for handouts. This allowed people in a community to show real love by helping each other, while making clear that laziness was no claim to other people's property.

Progressive, bureaucratic welfare programs are centralized in Washington, D.C., and state capitals and administered by professional bureaucrats like you, who usually know little or nothing about the personal circumstances in local communities. Further, bureaucrats and administrators who work at government agencies for the purpose of running welfare programs have a big incentive to add more people to the rosters of welfare recipients. More dependents added to the welfare rolls means more power, more responsibility, and bigger budgets for bureaucratic welfare program administrators. So your goal is not to help people get off government welfare, it's to help more people get on it.

ABLE-BODIED VERSUS DISABLED

Earlier forms of assistance often discriminated between the many who are able-bodied and the few who are truly disabled. People in a local community would usually know who among them was able to work and who was not, as well as who was willing to work and who was not. And, typically, able-bodied people were offered assistance, but only in exchange for work, while families and citizens of various communities almost always helped to care for those few who were truly disabled and incapable of working.

Many forms of modern, progressive, bureaucratic welfare have required no work at all. From anyone. Because assistance provided by government welfare programs is presented as a "right," something to which people are "entitled." An able-bodied American today can receive fully subsidized health care insurance, for example, paid for by other citizens, and never be asked to work. An American today can receive education, housing, food, and all kinds of other goods and services, all paid for by others, and never be asked to work in return.

TEMPORARY ASSISTANCE VERSUS A WAY OF LIFE

Earlier forms of assistance typically provided the bare minimum for survival, because it was temporary, which often meant eating meager meals and sleeping in a "poor house" that could be anything from a stand-alone structure to a basement of a local church to a farmer's barn. People who received earlier forms of assistance were highly incentivized to be productive and quickly leave the life of assistance because the life of assistance was unpleasant.

Progressive, bureaucratic welfare aims to provide assistance that equates to some kind of common American standard of living—because some kind of common American standard of living is now a "right," something to which all Americans are "entitled" and no longer something to be earned. This is why many advocates for government welfare programs argue endlessly that the poor, or others, deserve more entitlements from government. And more entitlements mean more job security for you, so you'll want to encourage the creation of new entitlement programs and the expansion of existing ones, and become a political cheerleader for those who advocate for the same.

VOLUNTARY VERSUS INVOLUNTARY GIVING

Earlier forms of assistance were usually voluntary. Those who gave did so because they wanted to give. Those who received assistance knew who was giving to them. It was natural for those who received to feel obligated to pay back to those who gave, someday, some way. No one, back then, thought that any kind of assistance (food, lodging, clothing, medicine, etc.) from anyone was any kind of right. Everyone understood that assistance was a gift and they appreciated whatever help they received. The feeling of obligation was yet more incentive for those receiving assistance to work productively so that they could pay back the debt they owed, or, at a minimum, so that those who received assistance could one day be in a position to give assistance to others.

Of course, in this old system, which was local and personal and voluntary, there was not much of a role for bureaucrats, which is an important reason why this old way of welfare was not good for you.

Progressive, bureaucratic welfare is emphatically *not* voluntary. Government policy commands it while bureaucrats enforce it. The law forces taxpayers to support progressive, bureaucratic welfare programs, whether individuals want to support those programs or not. The result? Those who give become ubiquitous, and therefore unknown. They become anonymous to those who receive.

Those who receive feel no obligation to pay anything back because they think the assistance they've received through government programs is their "right," something to which they are "entitled." Further, recipients don't even know who they owe, should they ever want to pay someone back.

LOVE

You probably never expected to read about "love" in a guidebook for bureaucrats and regulators, did you? Well, love used to be connected in an important way to programs of personal assistance for individuals in need. It no longer is, so it's worth mentioning in this survey of the differences between older ways versus modern bureaucratic ways of offering help to others.

Earlier forms of assistance for individuals were all about people helping friends and neighbors in times of temporary need, people helping others facing difficult, trying circumstances beyond their control: a fire, a flood, a crippling accident, a disease. These were acts of love and care.

They were also acts of mutual self-interest. A citizen was likely to help a neighbor who suffered great misfortune because that citizen knew that he might experience a bad run of luck someday and find himself in need of help from others. In a peculiar and beautiful way, older forms of assistance united self-interest with an interest in helping others. Those who received temporary help were usually better years later because of that assistance. And those who gave were better because they were helping others become better.

WEALTH CREATION

Prior to the New Deal, chronic poverty—meaning generation after generation of poverty within a family—was rare. Additionally, it did not constitute a claim for entitlements funded by fellow citizens. The reason is that early generations of Americans had discovered the solution to the problem of poverty: the freedom to create new wealth.

Early generations of Americans knew that wealth does not simply exist in the ether of the universe, waiting to be distributed among human beings by government or some other force. They knew that wealth must be created. They knew that human beings emerged into the world with no wealth at all, that the natural human condition is miserable poverty, that everything of economic value—from CT scans and X-ray machines to sturdy houses to safe cars to computers to smart phones to entertaining movies and more—has to be created, invented, and produced by someone.

They knew that as some individuals start to work productively and create new wealth, others can do the same, if they so choose and if they are free to do so. The total amount of wealth in the world is not fixed, or unchangeable. Wealth is not a zero-sum game. Some people creating wealth does not mean others must lose wealth or have it taken away. Individuals who create wealth by producing value actually inspire others to create wealth by producing value, because each wants to trade with the other. And as more people become productive, the total amount of wealth in the world increases.

Early generations of Americans also knew that wealth is created by producing something—a product, service, or experience—that others value, something that others want, need, or appreciate. Families who are busy creating wealth by producing value for others, in a civic environment of freedom and strict legal protections for private property, are not chronically poor. They're climbing the ladder of economic mobility and prosperity. Further, people who are busy creating wealth by producing value for others are people who tend not to be idle. They tend not to be prone to the many pathologies fueled by idleness.

In this way, older forms of assistance, from one community member to another, connected caring for each other with the civic conditions and personal encouragement to create wealth, escape poverty, and avoid destructive behaviors. People achieved this by staying busy producing value for neighbors, friends, and fellow citizens. But the results of the old ways of assistance don't matter for modern bureaucrats and regulators. Why?

Because for modern bureaucrats and regulators, results do not matter.

POLITICAL POWER

This is another important lesson for bureaucrats and regulators, whether you work for a government agency directly involved with providing assistance for individuals, or not. As a bureaucrat, the public and political justification for your position is that you help people in one way or another, either keeping them safe from various dangers or providing things (with other people's money) they want but don't have. No matter what your particular bureaucratic position is or will be, the lessons of modern American government welfare programs are instructive for you.

Modern, progressive, bureaucratic government welfare has had one main, hidden goal from its inception, far different than the publicized goal of helping people. That goal has been to increase power and control for those in government. It accomplishes this by offering different kinds of welfare assistance and taxpayer-funded subsidies to different constituencies in exchange for votes. Your role, as an unelected bureaucrat, is to regulate, confiscate, keep, and redistribute more and more private property and private wealth, which means controlling citizens to a large degree.

Let me clarify one point. There is no doubt that some individuals who have received progressive, bureaucratic welfare in times of need, have gone on to produce value for others and to prosper. That's happened. And that does not diminish the fact that the greatest beneficiaries of modern government welfare programs have been the politicians and bureaucrats who occupy seats of government power.

Recall that President Lyndon Johnson announced the "War on Poverty" in January of 1964. Since then, the United States government has spent more than $22 trillion of taxpayer money on anti-poverty programs. Trillion, with a *T*. When adjusted for inflation, that's more than three times the cost of all American military wars since the American Revolution.

Yet, what has happened to rates of poverty in the United States? Nothing. The percentage of poor Americans today is about the same as it was in 1964. Still, the numbers of bureaucrats fighting the War on Poverty and the power they exercise over others have grown exponentially during that same time period. See who really benefits from bureaucratic government programs?

The rise of progressive, bureaucratic welfare programs correlates with and likely has been a cause of the rise of all kinds of social pathologies. We've spent the better part of the past century building a sprawling, complex, national regulatory-welfare state—the very bureaucracy where you probably work right now or hope to work in the future—all in the name of helping children, poor people, women, racial minorities, and others. As those government programs expanded, incidents of domestic abuse went up, rates of drug and alcohol rates climbed, violent crime became more common, and the number of people suffering from mental health problems grew. But remember, results don't matter.

Who cares that as government spending and power expands, growing numbers of Americans become dependent on government programs and turn away from productive lives to live in idleness? In fact, notice the cycle that has developed. As government programs fuel more dependency, more idleness, and more pathologies, those in government and their voting supporters insist that the only possible remedies must include expansions of existing government programs or the creation of new ones. This leads to even more dependency, idleness, and pathologies. Which is great news for you, because it means that no one expects good results from your work, and when the results of your work are positively damaging and harmful, the demand for you will go up as more citizens clamor for increased government-managed assistance programs.

Government regulations almost never achieve their goals, which is why government regulations are almost never the cause of any social, technological, or environmental improvement. Nonetheless, virtually all Americans, when confronted with one failed regulation after another, after another, after another, will respond: "Yeah, those particular regulations might be wasteful, counter-productive, even positively harmful, but we still need *some* regulations." Americans are so foolish. They talk as if there's a real danger of running out of regulations. They clearly don't know that you and your government colleagues are cranking out tens of thousands of pages of rules and regulations every year.

As a bureaucrat, hopefully you see the value of this widespread social attitude. Americans never lose their faith in regulations or the bureaucrats who enforce them, no matter how bad the results are. Even in those rare moments when some critics question the merits of a regulation, you can offer the ultimate, irrefutable, discussion-ending justification for any government regulation, program, or policy: "Think of how much worse things would be without this government action!?"

Never stop reminding yourself that results don't matter. Only your intentions matter. As long as you can frame your intentions as morally superior to the intentions of your critics and opponents, you will prevail. Your budgets will expand. You'll get promotions and pay raises. Journalists and media wonks will heap praise on you. You'll become the subject that social scientists study and hold up as a model for students to study and emulate. You'll be granted more power over the lives and property of American citizens so long as you claim publicly that you want to help them, keep them safe, eliminate discrimination, and spread social justice. No one will care about or even pay attention to the actual results of your work. Ever. And the American people, many of whom cannot identify one regulation when asked, will continue to chant, as if part of some incantation, "we need regulations."

CHAPTER 7

YOU'LL MAKE EVERYTHING MORE EXPENSIVE, WHICH THE POOR WON'T LIKE, BUT IT'S FOR THEIR OWN GOOD

As a bureaucrat, the regulations you enforce on businesses will have one and only one certain effect: to make the products or services offered by the businesses *more expensive.*

The critics of modern bureaucratic government mentioned earlier, both the principled conservative Constitutionalists and the populists, will use this fact to build arguments and launch political attacks against your good work. They'll complain that markets provide better quality goods and services at lower prices, while government regulations and bureaucrats make everything more expensive. So let's step back and examine their argument. Let's see how markets work and why it's a good thing for you to regulate and control them.

WHAT HAPPENS IN A FREE MARKET

First, let's be clear about terms. The term "free market" is a misnomer and somewhat misleading. It is not one *thing*. In a decisive respect, there is no such thing as a "market." There are people. And people are either free or controlled. People are either free to do what they choose to do, to make what they want to make, to trade if and when and with whom they want to trade, or they are not.

When people are able to produce, interact, and exchange freely with others who want to produce, interact, and exchange with them, economists call that a "free market." The opposite of a free market is no market at all. The opposite of a free market is regulatory control and command, people being told what to do, when to do it, how, with whom, in what circumstances, under threat of punishment.

In a free market, or an environment of free enterprise not restricted by government regulation and interference, business owners typically try to attract as many customers as possible by providing the best quality products or services they can, at the lowest price. The challenge for any business is that competitors are always nipping at their heels, sometimes offering newer or better quality products or services, or lower prices, or both. The effects of competition are important features of any free market or free enterprise. Competition, combined with the incentive to make profits, results in the positive effects that come from free markets.

In an environment of free enterprise, in other words, where there is widespread demand for any product or service, the natural competitive pressures push toward higher quality products and services and lower prices. Higher quality and lower prices, over time, are the natural results of free markets and competition among and between businesses. The economic history of TVs offers a telling example.

LEARNING FROM SMART TVS

I recently took my 17-year-old daughter to pick out a TV for her bedroom. She was tired of fighting with her younger brothers when she wanted to watch television in the living room. We went to an electronics box store where we found a smorgasbord of new TVs. She wanted something relatively small. We ended up with a 32″ Smart HDTV with 1080p resolution. For a mere $200.

By way of historical comparison, in 1970, a 25″ color TV, which was considered big back then, and which was much lower quality than today's TVs, cost between $500 and $1000, depending on whether or not the TV came embedded in a gigantic, heavy wooden cabinet. Those were real prices, at that time. If we adjust for inflation and consider what a dollar then is worth now, the price of a 25" color TV in 1970 was between $3000 and $6000 in today's dollars. My parents can remember when only the rich families in town had a TV. Today, a mere generation later, most American households, rich and poor alike, boast one or more incredibly high definition, smart TVs.

So how did TVs come to be so much better, so much less expensive, so much more widely available to everyone, in such a short time? Answer: Widespread consumer demand fueled robust innovation and competition among TV engineers, manufacturers, and distributors, all in an environment of free markets, relatively unfettered by government interference, with few government regulations and few government subsidies.

Moreover, what happened with TVs happens with all kinds of technology. The TV example is evidence of a model, a set of principles that applies to all products and services that can be offered by some people and purchased (or declined) by others.

1. Where there's widespread demand for something within an environment of freedom, competition to provide that thing emerges, naturally.
2. Competition breeds excellence.
3. Excellence, in terms of products and services, means better quality and lower prices as time passes. Always.

This economic model arises from human nature. It is timeless and immutable, true always and everywhere, among all peoples. It applies to *all* goods and services that can be produced by some human beings and that are wanted, needed, or otherwise valued by others.

Most importantly: Competition, fueled by widespread demand, and leading to better quality, lower prices, and wider availability, is not the result of any government plan. It's the opposite. Competition, fueled by widespread demand, leading to better quality, lower prices, and wider availability, is due to the *lack* of a government plan. It's the result of free people producing and offering what other free people value, free from government control and regulatory restrictions.

AFFORDABLE TV ACT

Imagine if, sometime in the age of *All in the Family*, *Charlie's Angels*, or *Miami Vice*, Congress had passed an "Affordable TV Act," a government "plan" to subsidize TVs for select groups of citizens. It would have been easy to justify, after all. Imagine a politician proclaiming:

> TVs have become so important for communication, common news, and shared cultural entertainment experiences, that every American now has a "right" to an affordable, quality TV. Americans are entitled to an affordable, quality TV. And we in Congress will make sure every American gets their TV and that no American is left behind without a TV.

After passing an "Affordable TV Act," the federal government would've taxed many citizens heavily and used that money to subsidize TVs for others. What would have been the result? We know exactly what the result would've been, because we've witnessed what government subsidies do to industries like health care and education and farming and housing and many others. We've witnessed what government subsidies always do in all industries: drive up prices.

Under an "Affordable TV Act," many people who didn't really want or value a TV would buy one anyway simply because government would be footing the bill using taxpayers' money. A huge surge of money, in the form of subsidies, would instantly flow toward TV manufacturers, distributors, and sellers, not because of an increase in demand for TVs, but because government was all of a sudden spending other people's money on TVs.

TV manufacturers, distributors, and sellers would, in turn, raise their prices. Why? Because they could. Because government would be channeling loads of money to TV businesses in order to satisfy the alleged "right" of every American to an affordable, quality TV. If Uncle Sam is paying the bill, after all, why not raise the price?

Subsidies always lead to higher prices. Had there been an "Affordable TV Act" subsidizing TVs, their prices would have gone up, not down, and TVs quickly would have become too expensive, out of reach, and inaccessible for the average American lover of *Survivor* and *Jeopardy*.

Further, when taxpayer dollars subsidize TVs, manufacturers and distributors have little incentive to improve the quality of their TVs. What does it matter if the schmuck in the Barcalounger at home doesn't like the subsidized TV he's watching? He didn't pay for it, after all. And government would continue to subsidize TVs with taxpayer dollars, as part of the "Affordable TV Act," whether TV manufacturers improved the quality of their products or not.

TVS AND HEALTH CARE AND ALL OTHER PRODUCTS AND SERVICES

Had Congress passed an "Affordable TV Act" in the past, the result today would be crappy TVs that might cost $20,000 or $30,000 instead of the incredible, quality TVs we now see in stores for a few hundred bucks.

It's hard for many people to believe, and yet the truth remains: No matter what kind of products or services, we get better quality, lower prices, and wider availability so long as there is real demand (people wanting, needing, or otherwise valuing a commodity) and so long as there is an environment of real freedom, which means truly free markets and mutually agreeable, voluntary exchanges that are neither regulated nor subsidized.

We've seen that this is true for TVs. It's also true for health insurance, health care, and life-saving medicines and medical technology. It's true for housing, clothing, food, and education. It is true for every product or service, from antiperspirants to bagels to gym memberships, that people can produce or provide for others who value a product or service enough to pay for it.

Throw in government subsidies, however, add government regulations that create quasi-monopolies for some businesses by driving competitors away (ever heard of EpiPen?), toss in crony government perks and favors handed out to political friends, and everything changes. For the worse.

With increasing regulatory interference and taxpayer subsidies, markets become so distorted that the true market value of a product or service becomes unknowable. To anyone. Prices convey a wide range of important information to buyers, sellers, manufacturers, suppliers, and investors, about a product or a service, even an entire industry. Subsidies and regulatory restrictions, however, skew prices. The result is that no one can know truly how much demand there is, which makes it impossible to know how much supply to offer. As a result, the products and services that will be produced and offered for sale will be the most-subsidized products and services, not the products and services a market of people most value. Quality will decline. Prices will go up as more subsidy dollars chase after subsidized goods. This, too, is true for every commodity, including TVs. And health insurance. And life-saving medicines and health care. And housing, clothing, food, and education.

Americans today, fearful of what might happen if government subsidies for health care or other commodities are scaled back, are living a great irony. Entrepreneurs and manufacturers offer for sale the best cars, best houses and buildings, best medicines and health care, best food, best clothes, best communications technology, best of just about every imaginable thing, because there are still remnants of a free market in the United States. At the same time, however, many Americans believe they are "victims" of the businesses that research, develop, and offer for sale world-class goods. These are the kinds of Americans who clamor for more government control over just about every imaginable thing. Which means they want to give more power to you.

By demanding more regulations of some things and more subsidies for others, they aim to destroy the very conditions of freedom that fueled the creation of the many good things they now enjoy. They simply don't recognize this. They don't understand that they are undermining the very free market environment that produced the goods and services they now consider to be "rights" and "entitlements."

Meanwhile, in other parts of the world, millions of people live in miserable poverty, suffering from hunger, sickness, and short life spans. Many of those poor people live under the thumb of controlling, restrictive regimes that give lip service to the "right" to health care, as well as the "right" to housing, food, education, and many other goods. In many of the poorest countries in the world, such "rights" are written into their national constitutions. Yet there is little or no health care actually available, and little housing, food, or education, as those poor, sick, and dying people know all too well.

Those poor souls would love to have access to the goods Americans have, but they find it impossible to raise capital and research, develop, produce, and offer for sale such things because the government's heavy foot is always on their necks. Those poor souls fight to decrease the presence of government so that entrepreneurs might be free to invent and produce what others want, including quality medicines and health care.

If they're successful in getting rid of government regulations, subsidies, and control, and if they're productive and ambitious, someday they too will have stores full of low-priced, quality smart TVs. They'll also be able to buy the medicines, health care, and all kinds of other commodities, including antiperspirants, bagels, and gym memberships, they want, need, and value.

In point of fact, in nations around the world, wherever we see the beginnings of reducing government control, wherever we see small expansions of individual freedom and protections for private property, we see people starting to develop some kind of job skill, or learn some kind of training, even if they earn a mere pittance each day. For the poorest among the poor of the world, learning a skill and working each day for a dollar, or two, or three is often better than the alternative, which might be starving to death on a farm regulated top to bottom by government.

As people learn basic skills and begin to work entry-level jobs for a dollar or two per day, even in the poorest nations on Earth, they're increasing their productivity. Soon, others around them begin to produce more goods and services, so long as those others are relatively free to do what they want and keep what they earn. These people, who started life in the depths of poverty, are creating wealth by producing value for others. They are climbing their way out of poverty.

Nations begin poor. The first human beings in anthropologic history began poor. Some became wealthy. How? By *creating* wealth.

Two comprehensive online data sets are particularly useful in showing how many nations and millions of people, over long historical periods, live in conditions of poverty when they are not free to create and keep new wealth, while those who achieve some modicum of freedom often climb out of poverty by creating wealth. One is the Maddison Project, which was started by the economist Angus Maddison and has been continued by several of his students. The other is Gapminder, created by the statistician Hans Rosling. Exploring each of these data sets and using the research tools they make available is time well spent.

Or, if one is not interested in big, world-historical sets of data, one can look at a particular example, such as North and South Korea.

North Korea and South Korea are two nations right next to each other, both filled with millions of people of common ancestry. As recently as 75 years ago, the people of both North Korea and South Korea were universally poor by any standard. Really poor. Today, the people of North Korea remain really poor. Yet many people in South Korea are much wealthier than they were just a generation or two ago. Seoul is a beautiful, shiny, modern city featuring the most advanced technologies one can find. People in South Korea enjoy one of the highest per capita GDPs in all of Asia. South Koreans have one of the most highly educated workforces in the world. And economic opportunities for individual improvement are expanding.

So why are people in South Korea prospering while the people of North Korea—separated by a mere line in the dirt—so poor? Government power and control in South Korea has been scaled back, property rights are protected, and individuals are relatively free to do what they want and keep what they earn. And they worked and produced their way up the economic ladder, going from starvation-level poverty, to earning and producing a pittance each day, to earning and producing a little more, to earning and producing much more, to becoming one of the great economic powerhouses of the world.

We see examples of wealth creation, the conditions that incentivize wealth creation, and the human flourishing that follows, around the world and throughout history. And none of that is your concern. You are a bureaucrat-in-training. Your power base comes from Americans demanding that you control and regulate others by controlling and regulating markets. Your base of power comes from widespread distrust and suspicion among and between citizens.

The good news is that many Americans today clamor for more bureaucratic control over their fellow citizens and the businesses they operate, not less. Many American essentially demand the kinds of government control and regulation that other people in other parts of the world are trying to eliminate. Whatever that means for the American people, it certainly means more power and job security for you. It also means that the incredible progress that happened in the relatively free market of TVs won't happen in the many other markets you regulate and control. So don't expect the same results. Regulations are no substitute for competitive, free markets.

HOW REGULATIONS MAKE THINGS MORE EXPENSIVE

Government regulations disrupt the natural activities of markets. The reason is simple. Instead of businesses freely strategizing, researching, innovating, and figuring out ways to produce higher quality products and services at lower prices, regulations require that businesses do things according to regulations, not in ways that are innovative or efficient or best.

Government regulations often require businesses to submit reams of paperwork and data in order to be in "compliance." Often, businesses must hire full-time employees just to fill out all the forms required by government regulations. These employees are usually called "compliance officers." And their salaries add to the operating costs of a business.

How does a business pay for those salaries as well as all its other expenses? Often by raising the prices of the products and services it offers for sale to customers. That's one way regulations make things more expensive.

As a budding bureaucrat, you might be thinking to yourself: "Yeah, maybe some regulations make prices a little higher for some products and services, but not much, right?"

Wrong. Regulations increase prices a lot. Directly and indirectly, across the board.

One study, conducted by the United States Chamber of Commerce, found at least 34 federal regulations that each had direct, immediate compliance costs for businesses of at least $1 billion per year. Or more. That's only federal regulations, not state and not local. And that's only the regulations with an annual direct compliance price tag of $1 billion or more among the many tens of thousands of other regulations.

Another study, conducted by the National Association of Manufacturers, discovered that in 2012, federal regulations cost more than $2 *trillion*. And that was only regulations for manufacturing businesses.

Who paid that $2 trillion? Customers paid it, mainly. In the form of higher prices for all the manufactured products they bought, their fidget spinners and pick-up trucks and pet food. Shareholders also paid for it, in the form of lower returns on their investments. Employees also paid, in the form of lower wages and salaries.

No one knows with any certainty exactly how much government regulations cost consumers every year. No one *can* know. Why? Because no one knows how many regulations there are at the federal, state, and local levels in the United States, not to mention the millions of pages of rules generated to guide bureaucrats like you who administer the regulations and monitor other regulators.

More, it's impossible to calculate with precision the price or cost of regulations. In addition to the direct costs of compliance, for example, there are all kinds of indirect costs, such as the opportunity costs of what businesses might've or could've done with the capital they spent on regulatory compliance, or the innovative, inventive, productive work a compliance officer might've done if she had not spent all her time filling out regulatory forms. How does one put a price tag on such variables?

Suppose, as a thought experiment, that you were thinking about investing some of your money, which you earned through productive work, into research and development to invent a new medicine and bring it to market. Why might you want to make such an investment? Because you care about sick people and you want to help them, while earning a return on your investment at the same time.

On average, it takes 12 years or more for the United States Food and Drug Administration to approve a new medicine. Could you wait more than a decade before regulators allow you to try sell your medicine and make a return on your investment? How many people can afford to invest in any business plan that prohibits marketing and selling to potential customers for 10, 12, 15 years or more, especially when there is no guarantee that anyone will want to buy what the business has to sell once it is approved?

How many potential investors, because of the burden of FDA regulations, simply decide not to invest in research and development of new medicines? And how much does it cost—what is the price?—paid by the suffering of people who struggle with diseases or die because a medicine that might have been invented and cured them is never invented at all? How can we assign a dollar amount to their pain? It's impossible.

This problem is not peculiar to pharmaceutical businesses. It happens in all industries. A bank president in Denver, Colorado, reported that he spends four out of five business days per week, on average, focused not on improving the business of his bank, or helping current clients, or finding new clients, but on government regulations and regulators. And, to boot, he told me that his time was in addition to that of several full-time compliance officers who do nothing but focus on government regulations and regulators. How much more productive could that bank be—how many more small business loans, home loans, car loans, education loans, etc.—could that bank process if it was not spending so much time and money paying employees to deal with government regulations and answer to government regulators?

Consider also: When government regulations make the price of one product or service more expensive, how do people pay for that price increase? They have to charge more for their own products or their own labor. In other words, increases in the prices of some products and services caused by government regulations quickly lead to increases in the prices of many other products and services.

There's yet another cause for higher prices: simple bureaucratic creep, often wrongly confused with incompetence. But it's not necessarily incompetence. Very often, when bureaucrats are in charge of a program, they need the advice of other bureaucrats. That costs money and drives up price. Also, bureaucrats may not have time to select the most efficient contractors and sub-contractors to do a job. And they might here and there provide highly overpriced government contracts to crony friends or relatives—a subject explored in Chapter 13. And government jobs often get delayed, which drives up costs, because there's no incentive to finish anything on time or to meet goals or deadlines, the subject of Chapter 12.

The United States Department of Veterans Affairs, which is a model of a government-managed, single-payer health care system, offers an example of bureaucratic creep. The VA has become synonymous with higher prices and higher costs—including significant sums of money that sometimes just go missing without any explanations at all—while providing sub-standard health care services for American veterans essentially trapped in the VA system.

Years ago, VA bureaucrats proposed to build a new hospital on the outskirts of Denver, Colorado, a project approved by Congress. The original price tag for construction of the new hospital was $600 million. Still not completed as of the writing of this book, with delays now counted in *years*, the cost of the hospital has grown to at least three times the original: $1.8 billion. And that is merely as of now. It's still being built. No one really knows how high the costs might go, should the facility ever be finished and opened to serve veterans.

The point is that money has to come from somewhere, or be paid by someone. It's one example among many of how government makes things more expensive by wasting time, energy, and money. The VA effectively said, "We'll build a $600 million hospital for a mere $1.8 billion, or maybe more if we need it, and it will be finished sometime within a decade of the promised completion date."

For all these reasons and more, no one really knows how much regulations cost businesses, or cost customers, or cost everyone affected, directly or indirectly.

REGULATORS SHOULD NOT FEEL BAD

As a bureaucrat, you might be feeling a little bad right now. After all, it's not your intention to make everyone pay higher prices for the products and services that help improve their lives. But remember what we just learned in the last chapter: When it comes to government programs and regulations, results don't matter. Only your *intentions*, as a bureaucrat, matter.

The higher prices caused by government regulations affect everyone, but the poorest citizens feel the biggest impact. They, after all, have the fewest resources and the least disposable money, so when the prices of basic items such as food and clothing and medicines and housing go up, the poor don't like it. It makes their lives even more difficult.

Here it becomes important that you never forget the calling that led you to a career in government. You should never forget that you do not trust citizens, mainly because they don't deserve to be trusted. You know citizens will hurt each other, steal from each other, and rip each other off any chance they get. And the most vulnerable among us are the poor, who tend to be the least educated (despite the bureaucrat-conceived, government-administered, and government-monitored, single-payer, universal education system now available to all Americans).

Poor Americans are basically waiting to be taken advantage of by wealthy business owners and corporation shareholders. The only thing that stands between them and business predators—the only thing that prevents rich people from screwing over the poor—is you, the dedicated bureaucrat enforcing government regulations.

So it is true that the regulations you enforce as a bureaucrat will make everything more expensive. The poorest Americans won't like this very much. And principled conservative critics as well as populists will use these facts to launch political attacks against the regulatory agencies where you and other bureaucrats are building your careers. If you are challenged on this point by critics, don't try to refute them. Just change the topic. Mock them. Call them racist. Or compare them to Hitler.

Be prepared to remind your critics and everyone else that your *intention* is to protect the poor from the rich, protect everyone from their own bad decisions, and protect every group of Americans from every other group of Americans. Remember, results don't matter. Your good intentions justify everything you do. Because every group of Americans wants to hurt, cheat, or steal from every other group of Americans. Except bureaucrats. The intention of bureaucrats, or at least the publicly stated intention of bureaucrats, is to help others and keep them safe.

If you do your job well, if you enforce every regulation and rule to a "T" without exception—if you never let common sense stop you from following regulatory procedures—then likely you will receive special honors and awards bestowed by your fellow bureaucrats and supervisors. When you feel the pride of knowing you did a noble job well swelling in your throat, you'll know your efforts were not in vain. And the cheering of your government colleagues and the media and academicians—perhaps even a Hollywood movie will be made to celebrate your bureaucrat successes?—will drown out the lamentations of the poor as they complain about higher prices and no longer being able to afford the basics of life.

CHAPTER 8

INNOVATION BAD, REGULATIONS GOOD: KEEP DOING THINGS THE OLD WAY

*M*arket disruption is a synonym sophisticated people use for *innovation*. It's easy to see why. Innovation involves coming up with some new, better way of doing some kind of task or work. And any new, better way tends to displace or otherwise disrupt the old way of doing things.

Many examples of market disruption dot the historical landscape. In the 1880s and '90s, for example, one of the greatest and growing public health threats in the United States was horse poop. No joke. The Industrial Revolution of the 19th century led to American cities increasing in size. Never before had so many people lived in such close proximity to one another, with city populations exploding into the hundreds of thousands and eventually millions. This also meant large, unprecedented numbers of horses, the main vehicle for local transportation at that time, living in close proximity to one another. Which resulted in unprecedented volumes of horse waste.

Editorialists in city newspapers warned that the mounds of horse manure would soon be taller than city buildings. And this was not much of an exaggeration. People had no idea how to get rid of all the horse dung, which attracted insects, emitted dangerous gases, and contaminated water supplies. Horse poop was a growing and very serious public health problem in the United States, and no laughing matter.

Then along came Henry Ford, who saw a market for new transportation technology: a horseless carriage powered by an internal combustion engine. He solved the horse manure crisis, invented and produced something people valued, created an entirely new industry of jobs for those who wanted to work, and made a great fortune for himself and thousands of others in the process. Ford's productive innovation—figuring out how to mass produce automobiles for a price that enabled ordinary Americans to buy them—was a great disruption to the markets of buying, selling, and maintaining horses for the purposes of human transportation and parcel deliveries.

Another example of market disruption, also involving cars, and much more recent, is Uber.

Launched in 2009, Uber bypassed the entire industry of government-licensed taxis by connecting willing drivers and willing passengers through a smartphone app. Uber doesn't provide cars or drivers. Anyone with a valid driver's license and a car can be an Uber driver, and anyone willing to pay an agreed-upon rate can catch a ride. Uber drivers and riders rate one another for everyone else to see—riders are free to avoid drivers with bad reviews, and drivers are free to ignore requests from flaky riders. That's why many people love Uber.

Uber has proven to be a great disruption to the monopoly that government-licensed taxi companies once had over the entire industry of paying-for-a-car-ride in American cities. And that's why big city American taxi companies have responded by cleaning up their taxis, hiring better drivers, lowering their fares, and becoming more competitive in order to attract customers.

No, not really—that's a joke.

Big city taxi companies did none of those things. Instead, they went to court and tried to get judges, regulators, and bureaucrats to keep Uber out, or shut Uber down, or both.

We could list many more examples of market disruptions, hundreds and thousands, in every industry and profession that now exists or ever has existed, yet the story in each would be the same, because the principle of disruptive innovation is the same everywhere and always.

REGULATIONS AND INNOVATION DON'T GO TOGETHER

Innovation introduces something new and therefore different than what is old, different than what has become the status quo. Innovation necessarily represents a challenge to the old way things have been and continue to be done. That's why innovation is a form of disruption.

By understanding the intrinsic connection between innovation and disruption, you can understand better why regulations and innovation don't mesh. And why your job, as a bureaucrat enforcing regulations, is more important than ever.

Government regulations are part of the larger progressive purpose to create a society that is designed by scientific experts, managed, planned. No group of people has more faith in intelligent design than government regulators and the progressive voters who support them.

For example, think of the pride progressive Americans have today living in "planned communities." Nothing is left to chance. A designer—or, more likely, an unelected board of social engineers—sits down and plans everything about a community: a park with government-approved safety playground equipment there, a police station over there, a school near here, some businesses way over there where the damage they cause will be minimal, taxpayer-subsidized commuter trains and bike paths to connect the parts of the city. Planned communities are examples of the progressive spirit of living in a highly-regulated environment where intelligent experts design everything.

Government regulations, in other words, are the opposite of social chaos. Free markets and innovative market disruptions *are* social chaos. It's a simple argument:

1. Unregulated, free markets mean competition.
2. Competition means innovations.
3. Innovations mean unplanned disruptions.
4. Unplanned disruptions mean social chaos and anarchy.

Just connect the premise, 1, to the conclusion, 4, and the problem becomes clear. Unregulated, free markets lead to social chaos and anarchy.

People cannot be safe in an environment of social chaos and anarchy. So, what is the only obvious solution? What is the only way people can live in safe, orderly, planned, and controlled societies? Answer: Government regulations enforced vigorously by you.

Regulations and innovation are incompatible in a number of ways. To be clear, innovation is virtually inseparable from unregulated, free markets. Why else would anyone invest time, money, effort, and other resources trying to innovate and figure out better ways of doing something unless they were free to compete with other businesses that are still doing things the old ways? Where one finds unregulated, free markets, one finds much innovation. Which also means one finds much social chaos and therefore many social dangers.

The good news for you is that the opposite is also true: Where one finds many regulations, where markets and people are not free, one finds little innovation. One finds stability. Certainty. Social control and order.

Compare highly regulated taxis from the example above to mostly unregulated Uber business. Where prices are fixed by regulations, and bureaucrats tell taxis where they must form lines to pick up passengers, such as at airports and hotels, and what kinds of services they can offer, cabbies have no incentive to spruce up their taxis or in any way try to distinguish themselves from other taxi companies or other taxi drivers. Regulations make it so that each taxi driver will get as many customers as the other drivers, and be paid exactly the same amount, whether their taxi is clean or filthy, whether the driver is pleasant or creepy, whether the ride is enjoyable or miserable for the customer.

That means there will be little or no disruptive innovations in the government-licensed taxi industry. That also means public order, control, and safety because regulators and bureaucrats have planned and now control the taxi industry.

What about the free-market-based Uber? What might some Uber drivers do to be competitive? How might some Uber drivers try to attract more customers? Will some smile more? Clean up their cars? Offer to play the music riders enjoy? Offer discounted prices? And what will riders do to become preferred by Uber drivers? Tip more? Be courteous to drivers? Write good reviews of good drivers on social media?

The answer to all these questions is: No one knows for sure. That's why unregulated, free markets are so chaotic, so anarchical. Unregulated markets are so unplanned. Which is highly dangerous, very risky. Which is why we need more bureaucrats. Like you.

REGULATIONS REMOVE INDUSTRIES FROM DANGEROUS FREE MARKETS

Every highly regulated industry and profession operates outside of markets. One common way that bureaucrats remove entire industries from actual markets is by licensing. From lawyers to physicians, accountants to construction workers, even florists to hair stylists, there are many industries in which someone cannot compete without licensed permission from bureaucrats. Also, public utilities such as power and water companies and "public-private partnerships" of all kinds operate outside the realm of market-based systems.

In these industries and more, open, free, innovative competition is not only *not* encouraged, it's positively prohibited by government. Often with criminal sanctions. Cut and sell a flower without a government license, for example, or offer a new treatment for people who suffer from back pain without government approval, or do some landscaping in a customer's yard without the right government permit, and you might find yourself paying a fine or even going to jail.

In many ways, regulation and licensing are merely synonyms for government-created monopolies, the subject of the next chapter. The important thing to note here is that regulations of all kinds (and the monopolies they create) discourage disruptive innovations by restricting competition. Big, established businesses invite regulations and licenses precisely because they know that regulations will mean fewer competitors. As the economist Milton Friedman observed many years ago: "The pressure on legislatures to license an occupation rarely comes from the members of the public...On the contrary, the pressure invariably comes from the occupation itself." In the case of Uber, big city taxi companies went directly to their respective City Halls complaining: "You can't allow people to hire drivers who aren't *licensed* to provide a ride across town!"

As we have discovered, less competition means less innovation. Which is a good thing, right? After all, if regulations are good, and regulations are incompatible with innovation, then innovation must be bad. Which it is. Innovation is not merely disruptive, it is chaotic and anarchical, and therefore risky and dangerous. And those dangers outweigh whatever incidental benefits or improvements might happen every now and then because of innovations.

Regulations solve the problem of innovative disruptions by commanding businesses to do things the old way, to maintain the status quo as required by regulations, rather than doing things in innovative, disruptive ways. The more you enforce regulations, therefore, the more you will be helping to maintain the status quo, protecting Americans from the disruptive chaos and danger that comes with innovation.

Remember also that even when human progress happens by way of accidental, disruptive market innovations, or inventions, or technical advancements, there's no reason why bureaucrats, regulators, and politicians shouldn't take credit.

- Sure, rates of child labor went down and more children started attending schools when free, entrepreneurial people, motivated by the incentive to keep what they produced, began to be more productive and created enough wealth that they no longer needed the labor of their children. But bureaucrats, regulators, and politicians can claim it was all because of child labor laws and regulations. And the Department of Education.

- Sure, for thousands of years and up until very recently the practice of medicine hurt or killed far more people than it helped. Until investors, driven by the incentive to make profits, began funding, researching, and developing new medicines and medical practices. But bureaucrats, regulators, and politicians can claim it was all because of the FDA.

- Sure, the air and water got dirtier as the Industrial Revolution began, and then the air and water got cleaner as innovators and inventors developed newer and better industrial technologies that produce far less pollution. But bureaucrats and regulators and politicians can claim it was all because of the EPA.

See the pattern? It's okay, it's even advisable, for you, as a bureaucrat, to take credit for the good results made possible by the entrepreneurial, innovative, and productive work of others. Because even though they are the real reasons for social, technological, and environmental improvements, they're still shady, sneaking, corrupt human beings. And as we discussed in Chapters 1 and 2, they don't deserve to be trusted. Someone needs to watch and monitor and regulate them. That someone is *you*. And if taking credit for the good results that others made happen helps to keep you in a position of power, where you can regulate the lives and actions and property of citizens, then it's good. It's well worth the lie. Because after all, the ends truly do justify the means.

CHAPTER 9

COMPETITION BAD, REGULATIONS GOOD: IT'S A JUNGLE OUT THERE

In the previous chapter, you learned how you can help to maintain the status quo and protect people from social anarchy by creating intelligently designed, well-planned, controlled, and managed communities, while minimizing disruptive innovations, inventions, and dangerous new technologies, all by enforcing government regulations. You learned that one important way regulations limit innovation is by restricting competition.

That's not the only good that comes from regulatory restrictions of competition. Competition poses far more dangers to the public than merely fueling innovations, efficiencies, and new technologies, especially when people come to rely too much on competition and forget about the importance and goodness of government regulations. This chapter, therefore, provides yet more reasons why it's good for bureaucrats to restrict competition through the power of government regulations.

MYTH OF THE INVISIBLE HAND

From the time of Adam Smith to today, misguided economists and philosophers have foolishly believed that unregulated, free markets of thousands or millions of people, each making individual choices about how to use their labor and resources and what to buy and trade, can somehow, almost magically, lead to improvements for those many people. This is what Mr. Smith called the "invisible hand" of free markets, and the name he chose was more appropriate than he probably knew. The "hand" guiding free markets is invisible, it cannot be seen, after all, because it's not real. There is no "invisible hand." It does not exist.

Competition in open markets leads to unfair advantages, opportunistic gains, growing income gaps between rich and poor, and obscene profits for a greedy few at the expense of the naïve, mostly ignorant poor masses who get swindled, cheated, or otherwise ripped off (and who elect politicians). Or worse. Often, in a free market, the naïve, ignorant masses pay with their health or even their lives for the dishonest, misleading, and falsely advertised schemes of the greedy few who will happily sell death and destruction labeled as toys and medicines if regulators don't intervene.

We discussed the reason in Chapter 1. The vast majority of human beings (other than bureaucrats, of course) are dishonest and untrustworthy. Human beings, by nature and by social conditioning, are self-serving, looking to help themselves by hurting or stealing from others. That's why we need regulators and bureaucrats. We are so lucky that people like *you* don't possess the same nefarious human nature or suffer from the same suspect social conditioning as other human beings. It's almost as if human nature has evolved into two separate species: regular human beings, who are nasty to one another and in need of regulation and control, and superior human beings, who are here to provide that regulation and control for the regular people.

People look for conflict because conflict provides opportunities for hurting other people. And what is competition but a form of conflict? When people compete with others, they look for any way possible to win, which often means looking for any way to hurt or even destroy their opponent. Competition, in other words, does not reveal the best in people. It reveals the worst.

SPORTS

Consider, as an example, the highly competitive arena of sports, amateur or professional. Sports are, by design, competitive. That competition goads players and teams to practice, strategize, work, and try hard to beat opposing teams or players. It also fuels widespread cheating, drug use, and other ways of winning outside the rules.

Let's be honest. When a team wins a big championship—think of the Superbowl, or the World Series, or the NCAA College Basketball Championship or the NBA Championship—it has little to do with hard work, determination, or persistence, much less good character, innovation, or intelligence. It's about cheating. Competition is merely another way of saying that everyone cheats and the winners are those who don't get caught. *That's* the result of competition.

Wouldn't high school football programs, for example, produce fairer football if we eliminated competition altogether by removing the incentive to outscore opponents and greatly increasing football regulations? Imagine how much better football would be if regulators commanded and controlled in detail how each team practiced, and how players ran each play during games, down to the details of how each quarterback throws, each receiver catches, or each defensive end blocks. Football would become so much fairer, and we could eliminate the victory gap between winners and losers, if every player was forced to play the game in exactly the same way, according to uniform and detailed regulations enforced vigorously by bureaucrats, while no scoring would be allowed for each game.

BUSINESS

Let's consider something more important than games: *business*. When businesses offer products and services for sale to the public, how can people know if they are safe or reliable? How can they know if the products or services actually are what they are advertised as being? How can anyone know if a tool, for example, works the way a company says it will work, or that something labeled as a medicine is not really a worthless placebo in disguise, or maybe even poison?

There are two common answers to these questions, and the answers are opposed to and incompatible with one another: *competition* versus *regulations*.

Pie-eyed optimists believe that competition among businesses is the way to get the best doctors and nurses, the best teachers and engineers, the best foods, the best communications technologies, the best standards for building homes and other structures, and all around the best products and services of all kinds. These air dreamers believe, naïvely, that there exists an indissoluble union between competition and excellence, such that one cannot exist without the other.

These same fools think that competition among businesses, within an unregulated, free market, will lead to many people making choices among and between those competing businesses. They blindly trust that the urge to satisfy customers will cause each business to try its best to provide the best products and services possible. Further, these same wearers of rose-colored glasses trust that the free market will punish businesses that deceive, cheat, or hurt customers. These people, who have drunk deeply from the intoxicating well of extreme free market economic theory, actually believe that free people will freely choose on their own to stop buying from businesses that sell products that harm, hurt, or maim. So dangerous. So naïve.

The problem with this approach is that its advocates do not fully understand how stupid and irresponsible ordinary human beings are. Seriously, how many people are truly smart enough to be responsible for their own choices and decisions? Especially about products, services, and subjects about which they know little? Most people simply do not have the brains to choose, on their own, or even with help from friends and family members, what to eat, what medicines to take when sick, what school is best for their children, or even what brand of light bulbs to buy. And we all know it.

Further, this view of trusting free markets and free people making their own choices fails to take into account the single greatest interest of each and every business: to steal what belongs to fools. Businesses exist to trick customers into exchanging cash for products or services that are worth much less than the advertised price. That's how businesses make profits, after all. The more profits a business records, the more that business has swindled and misled people. So it's in the interest of every business to conceal the ways it deceives others. Which is why we cannot trust people to know when they're being deceived and make choices accordingly. Ordinary people making their own choices simply are no match for professional teams of deceptive marketers and slick advertisers hired by businesses.

REGULATIONS MORE EFFECTIVE THAN COMPETITION

That points to the alternative, second way of making sure that businesses provide the products and services they claim to provide, of making sure that businesses help customers rather than hurt them, make them sick, or even kill them: government regulations.

Regulations keep businesses honest and in line by requiring that they comply with...regulations. That's obvious. Of equal importance, however, and perhaps less obvious, is the effect regulations have on competition. There is an inverse relationship between regulations and competition: Where there are more regulations, there's less competition. And where there are fewer regulations, there's more competition.

With more regulations come more costs to businesses, as discussed in Chapter 7. Regulations drive up start-up costs, operating costs, opportunity costs, and compliance costs for businesses. These increasing costs cause many existing businesses to close because they cannot make a profit. Higher costs also deter many investors and entrepreneurs from even attempting to start a new business. All of this means that regulations lead to fewer businesses. And fewer businesses means less competition for the businesses that survive. It is not unusual for the largest corporations in an industry to have the staff and resources to absorb the costs of regulations and the burdens of compliance. Big businesses, in other words, are often the only ones that can endure the increasingly high costs of regulations. Small businesses often cannot afford the costs of regulatory compliance. Which means regulations help the biggest businesses by reducing the number of competing smaller businesses.

As an example of how regulations simultaneously reduce and replace competition, consider the sprawling Dodd-Frank Wall Street Reform and Consumer Protection Act. Between late 2010, when President Obama signed Dodd-Frank into law, and early 2017—just over six years—only 20 new, small community banks opened in the United States. Meanwhile, during those same six years, more than 1200 community banks closed their doors for good.

Why were so many community banks closing at the same time that almost no new ones were opening? Because the compliance costs of Dodd-Frank make it virtually impossible to start a community bank without gigantic up-front capital investments. And the same compliance costs forced many existing community banks out of business. Their profit margins were already thin; they simply did not have the capital or labor to comply with the regulatory costs and burdens that Dodd-Frank imposed.

Community banks going belly up was the tip of the iceberg. When they shut their doors, their employees lost their jobs. Additionally, small businesses that desperately needed loans from their local community bank had nowhere to go for financing. Many of those small businesses closed their doors as well, unable to get the capital they needed to continue to operate.

As those hundreds of community banks have closed, who has benefited the most? Answer: The largest banking corporations in the United States. They now have to compete with far fewer banks. The high regulatory costs of the Dodd-Frank Wall Street Reform and Consumer Protection Act, including arbitrary fines and punishments dished out by bureaucrats at the Federal Consumer Financial Protection Bureau, have essentially created a monopoly of the biggest banking corporations in the United States.

But that's okay for you, Mr. or Ms. Bureaucrat. In fact, it's good news. Because as we'll see in Chapters 13 and 15, the few large corporations that benefit the most from the regulations you enforce are quite willing to pay large sums of money to politicians, bureaucrats, and regulators to keep increasing the regulatory burdens that drive out competing businesses. Which means lots of money and power and prestige all being directed at you. Yay!

CHAPTER 10

RESPONSIBILITY BAD, REGULATIONS GOOD: WHO ME? I WAS FOLLOWING REGULATIONS

The subject of responsibility brings up another important contrast between old-fashioned Constitutional laws and progressive regulations. In particular, the basic idea of tort law and the principle of individual responsibility enshrined within it, and the basic idea of regulations, are incompatible with each other. And you will be well-served to understand how and why they're incompatible, so that you can better respond when faced with businesses and other groups using regulations to shield them from being held responsible for some damage they caused.

The premise of tort law is the very old-fashioned, non-progressive notion of individual responsibility. Regulations, however, are much more sophisticated, much more progressive. The premise of regulations is that most individuals are too stupid, too incompetent, or too corrupt to be responsible for their own choices and actions. Which they are. That's why regulations effectively replace individual responsibility under the laws.

TORT LAW

The English words "tort" and "torture" share the same Latin root. In law, a "tort" is simply an act or omission that causes harm to another. A tort is some kind of wrongful damage caused by one person, either knowingly or unknowingly, to another person.

Tort law is a way to provide relief for those wrongs. It effectively says to people: "Live freely, make your own choices, and do whatever you want with whatever is yours, but beware. If you are responsible for causing damage to others, whether knowingly or unknowingly, you will have to repair whatever damage you cause."

Tort law, in other words, encourages people to be careful about their own actions and how they use their own property because they know that if they hurt someone or damage someone's property, they will be responsible for repairing that damage and making the victim whole again, as far as possible with material resources. In this way, tort law combines individual freedom, individual responsibility, and a kind of justice for those who are wrongfully harmed by others.

Which is another way of saying the premise of tort law is individual responsibility. And the assumption of tort law is freedom. That is, people are assumed to be free, and therefore they are held responsible when they use their freedom to damage others. According to the idea of tort law, there is to be no punishment and no reparation *until* and *after* someone is responsible for hurting or causing damage to another. Tort law has no application when no one is causing damage to others. When no one is injuring anyone else, people simply live freely and do whatever they please with whatever is their own, however and whenever they choose.

REGULATIONS

The premise of regulations is strikingly different. From the point of view of regulations, human beings cannot safely be trusted to be free, make their own choices, live as they please, or do what they want with whatever is theirs—especially not their own business. This suspicion of people springs from the low bureaucratic view of human nature, which we've already discussed: Human beings are inherently hurtful, destructive, and dishonest.

The premise of tort law, from the progressive point of view of bureaucratic regulators, is naïve and foolish. Tort law, from a regulator's perspective, means waiting for disasters to happen and then looking for inadequate ways to remedy the damage, when it's too late.

Stated succinctly, tort law is an example of the assumption that people should be presumed innocent until proven guilty. But regulations, as we already saw in

Chapter 2, enshrine the idea that most people are guilty and therefore should be presumed guilty until they prove their innocence.

Regulations are a form of prior restraint. Rather than waiting until someone causes damage or does something wrong, regulations restrain people *before* they have the opportunity to cause damage or do wrong. That's why you, the bureaucrat, don't regulate only those people who cause wrongful damage to others. Rather, you regulate everyone who falls under your jurisdiction, including the vast majority of people who have never been caught doing wrongs or causing damage of any kind. You regulate people before they do damage.

Think about it: The vast majority of the many people you regulate, including business owners, property owners, parents, children, researchers, educators, and professionals in all kinds of industries, have never been proven guilty of causing damage or doing wrongs, and yet you regulate them and compel them with threats of government punishment to demonstrate to your satisfaction, every reporting period, that they are in compliance with the regulations you enforce.

REGULATIONS DISPLACE RESPONSIBILTY

Regulations have, to a large degree, displaced tort law. And, to a corresponding degree, regulations have displaced the meaning of individual responsibility in the law.

It's likely that someday soon we will have nothing but regulations, and no tort law at all, as they are incompatible in principle with each other. Choosing one really does mean *not* choosing the other. To borrow a phrase made famous by Abraham Lincoln, regulations and tort law within one legal system represent a "house divided against itself."

The more bureaucrats like you who regulate the lives and property of Americans—the more detail with which you regulate their homes, businesses, foods, medicines, education, religion, and speech—then the less responsible Americans are for anything they do. Right? After all, how can an American citizen be responsible for doing something when bureaucrats command her to do it, and tell her how to do it, and when to do it, and even why to do it?

It might come as a surprise to some bureaucrats and the citizens who support them to learn that in spite of mountains of government regulations, there are still accidents, negligence, and purposeful damage caused by some business owners. You've been reading this book, so you now know the secret that for bureaucrats and regulators, results don't matter. Still, many bureaucrats have found plausible justifications for multi-million-dollar research projects that study accidents, injuries, and damage happening in spite of regulations. Taxpayers fund these research projects, of course, which usually requires hiring yet more bureaucrats to conduct the research needed to discover that other bureaucrats failed to prevent accidents and intentional injuries.

While the results of that research are pending, what happens when customers or even the public accuse a business, especially a large, highly regulated corporation, of a serious wrong? The first response from the accused corporation is, "Who, us? We were simply following regulations! We were doing what bureaucrats commanded us to do. We are not and cannot be responsible for damage that's been caused by doing things as ordered by government regulators."

This happened, for example, after the BP Deepwater Horizon oil spill in the Gulf of Mexico. It happened after large-scale, damaging scandals were discovered at Enron, AIG, Lehman Brothers, and Goldman-Sachs. And others. Business owners, corporate CEOs, and often their crony politician friends in government, immediately following any significant accidental or even purposeful damage, typically point to government regulations and regulators as the responsible parties.

And those business owners and corporate CEOs have a point. Why should they be held responsible for their actions when their actions were dictated in detail by government regulations? In short, the more power government exercises over citizens, the more responsibility government has for what happens among and between citizens. And the more responsibility government has for what happens among and between citizens, the less responsibility can be attributed to those citizens.

This is important for you to know. As a bureaucrat, it should be a sobering lesson. Yes, in controlling virtually every area of human life in the modern United States, you will become quite powerful. At the same time, with that power comes responsibility. People will increasingly point accusing fingers at *you*, the bureaucrat, because they might believe you are to blame when things go wrong. And they certainly will be happy to attribute great responsibility to you if that provides a way for them to shirk responsibility when they've done wrong or caused damage to someone else.

But fear not. Even if you failed in your mission as a bureaucratic regulator, there is a perfectly good and sound reason for your failure. The reason is that you did not have adequate resources to do your work properly. This provides you, my bureaucrat friend, with an opportunity to demand more resources and more authority so that in the future, the kind of disaster that happened under your regulatory watch will "never happen again."

PART
III

INCENTIVES
FOR A
BUREAUCRAT

CHAPTER 11

YOUR INCENTIVE TO PLEASE YOUR SUPERVISOR, NOT CITIZENS

T his is a good time for a quick review and overview of what it means as well as what it does not mean to be a bureaucrat in the United States today. For all bureaucrats and regulators, the better you understand the nature of your position and the purpose of the work you do, the better you'll understand how to pursue and make the most of the incentives available to you.

First and foremost, being a bureaucrat means you don't own a private business nor are you employed by one. All of the incentives, concerns, and motivations, all of the risks and potential rewards in a typical private business, do not apply to you. There are no customers willing to pay a market price for what bureaucrats have to offer (at least not openly, where others can see them paying bureaucrats). You have no customers in the traditional sense. Period.

You are a bureaucrat working within the vast machinery of modern government in the United States. You cannot create wealth for yourself by producing products or services or experiences that others value. There is no profit incentive available to you. You have no reason to allocate your capital in the most strategic ways, minimize the costs of your productivity, or maximize the revenue it generates, because you don't have capital or costs, you produce nothing, and you have no revenue other than your government salary, which is determined by other bureaucrats above you and beyond your control, not by the market demand for and market value of your talent.

At the same time, as a bureaucrat, you're not an elected politician. You're not an elected member of Congress or an elected President. You're not an elected state legislator or an elected governor. You're not an elected member of a county commission, or a city council, or a school board. You're not an elected sheriff or mayor. To a large extent, it does not matter much what voting citizens think of you or your performance at work.

If you spend time and energy trying to make voting citizens happy, you are wasting your time and energy. Seriously. You're wasting it. Why? Because voting citizens are not part of the bureaucratic process by which you can climb the ladder of success, get promotions, garner more power over more people, or earn pay raises along the way. Pay no attention to citizens or voters. They're irrelevant to your career.

YOU CAN'T BE FIRED

It's important to understand that as a bureaucrat in the United States government today, you effectively have life-tenure. It is almost impossible for anyone to fire you, for any reason. Ever.

Oh, there are obscure procedures buried in old laws and regulations and internal agency rules about how bureaucrats can be reprimanded, demoted, and even terminated for poor performance. But it virtually never happens. In the year 2015, as an example, among the several millions of non-military bureaucrats employed by the federal government, only 0.18% of the federal workforce were fired for poor performance or bad conduct. Less than 1%. Way less.

Think about that. That's only one or two bureaucrats out of a thousand who are fired for poor performance or bad conduct. Bureaucrats are, of course, as you know, a higher class of human being than the average citizen. But still. No private business and no industry has such a low rate of firing poorly performing employees as government. So why do so few bureaucrats get fired? Is it because of their superiority? In part, perhaps. But also because government agencies and offices feature disincentives for bureaucrats to hold other bureaucrats accountable, much less reprimand or fire them.

A recent investigation of federal government agencies in Washington, D.C., for example, found that large numbers of bureaucrats wasted oodles of time at work watching porn on their government computers. A bureaucrat at the EPA said he watched porn up to six hours per day for several years, all while at work. Another, at the Department of Commerce, connected to porn websites more than 1800 times while at work. Yet another bureaucrat, at the Federal Railroad Administration, was recorded surfing porn for more than 250 hours, while at work, in less than a year. None of these employees were fired.

Heck, even when there are so-called government shutdowns, not one bureaucrat typically loses his or her job. And, often, bureaucrats end up getting back pay after the shutdown is over and the government has re-opened. Give that some thought. Is there any other organization that can cease doing business, even temporarily, without one employee losing their job or missing a paycheck?

With the possible exception of tenured academics, most of whom work at taxpayer-funded schools and government-managed colleges and universities, nothing else comes as close to a permanent job for life as being a bureaucrat. You have chosen your future path wisely, grasshopper bureaucrat. You can do almost anything you want; you can be as lazy, irresponsible, dishonest, even abusive, as you want, and you almost certainly will never be fired from your government job. So go ahead: Steal from your office. Spend your work day surfing porn or social media on government computers. Have sexual relations with your colleagues. Show up drunk or stoned. Heck, don't show up at all.

No matter what you do or don't do, the supervising bureaucrats above you would prefer any course of action over trying to fire you, or even reprimanding you, because any attempt to reprimand or fire you would simply open them up and make them vulnerable to accusations of discrimination, or creating a hostile work environment, or violating one or more of the thousands of regulations that dictate how government offices and agencies must be run. Bureaucrats know better than anyone that it's impossible to navigate the labyrinth of government regulations, which is why every bureaucrat avoids that labyrinth as much as possible

Any bureaucrat who tries to reprimand or fire another bureaucrat is inviting a world of legal, regulatory, and professional trouble, which is why hardly any bureaucrats ever attempt it. After all, every bureaucrat knows that he or she will get paid the same whether misbehaving fellow government employees are reprimanded or fired, or not. So why would any supervisor jeopardize his or her cozy bureaucratic position and steady paycheck by trying to make other bureaucrats improve their performance, or by firing the worst of them? Bureaucrats have little incentive to care about the performance of other bureaucrats or an entire bureaucratic agency.

YOUR SUPERVISOR: THE KEY TO MOVING UP

Some bureaucrats might be satisfied with the government job they have right now, the rank they have, their current pay and benefits. Some have no desire to move up within the bureaucracy. And they are the bureaucrats typically most thankful that they cannot be fired, because they have no incentive to impress anyone in order to get promoted—they're not looking to get promoted.

But there are others, perhaps like you, who *do* want to move up within the bureaucracy. You're not going to be satisfied, after all, being paid as a GS-5, or GS-7, or GS-9. Nor will you be satisfied with the limited power that comes with the lower ranks. You want more. More money. More power. More control over others. So you can do more good, of course.

The question is: How you do get more as a bureaucrat? How do you climb the ladders of power and success and higher pay within government bureaucracies? Who must you impress or make happy?

The answer is key to your entire career. It's not customers. It's not voters. It's not taxpayers or citizens. The person whose derriere you must kiss the most and the best is your bureaucratic supervisor.

As a bureaucrat, your supervisor has enormous control over your career. So much control that if she doesn't like you, it really doesn't matter if you do your job well, or whether you follow the rules or procedures that apply to you. If your supervisor is not on your side, it won't matter if you achieve any particular goals, objectives, or outcomes. What matters—the only thing that really matters—is that you impress your supervisor so that she recommends you for promotions and salary increases.

Your strategy is clear: You do whatever makes your supervisor happy. Period. No questions asked. You do anything that is likely to cause your supervisor to recommend raises and promotions for you. And you refrain from doing anything that would cause your supervisor to consider not recommending you for raises and promotions.

- Suppose your supervisor comes to you and requests that you destroy, alter, or "lose" government documents? You do it.
- Suppose your supervisor asks you to lie about how your fellow bureaucrats do their jobs so that your supervisor looks better to her supervisor? You do it.
- Suppose your supervisor asks for personal favors, including sexual favors, drugs, stolen property, or anything else, on or off the clock? You do it.
- Suppose your supervisor demands that you use the full power of your government position as a bureaucrat to harass a private citizen who happens to be your supervisor's former lover? You do it.

- Suppose your supervisor suggests that you expedite approval for a government contract with a business owned by her brother? You do it.

See the pattern? You do *whatever* satisfies your supervisor and puts a smile on her face. Including making other bureaucrats in the nearby cubicle look bad, so that you look better by comparison in your supervisor's eyes. Do your best to learn what your supervisor does not like, or does not appreciate, and either avoid doing those things or conceal them well so that your supervisor never knows. That's the path to upward mobility within a bureaucracy.

Forget whatever you might have learned in any public administration classes in college. The purpose of those classes (and the entire academic discipline of public administration, for that matter, and most of academic political science) is simply to make ordinary citizens believe that big government bureaucracies were designed and continue to be administered by "experts."

Well, the truth is that public administration is not really a "science" in any serious meaning of the word. More importantly, the modern academic social sciences have little to do with your actual career as a bureaucrat. Getting ahead as one among millions of bureaucrats is a matter of persuasion, flattery, and seduction, maybe with a little bribery strategically offered here and there. You must combine these arts of personal advancement with the ability to read an "org chart" and identify which bureaucrats supervise which other bureaucrats, so that you can know which bigwigs to kowtow to in order to climb fast and high and achieve as much power over others as possible while receiving a big salary for your bureaucratic service.

CHAPTER 12

YOUR INCENTIVE TO FAIL

ailing to learn the important lesson of failing can be catastrophic for a bureaucrat's career. And as simple as this lesson sounds, failing requires practice, exercise, and training. Failing goes against human nature. And it's easy to forget. If you let your mind drift while at work inside your government office cubicle, and you don't pay attention, out of sheer unconscious habit you might start to achieve goals or reach objectives. All bureaucrats, young and old (but especially the young), seasoned and newbie (but especially the newbie), benefit from being reminded: *You must fail.*

The reason you must fail becomes clear once you understand the bureaucratic incentive to fail, an incentive created by the process of how money and power grow within a bureaucracy or regulatory agency. At the federal level, each and every government regulatory agency and bureaucratic department is created by an act of Congress.

- The Environmental Protection Agency, for example, was created by the 1970 Clean Air Act and subsequent Clean Water Act.

- The Consumer Products Safety Commission was created by the 1972 Consumer Products Safety Act.
- The Federal Department of Labor was created in 1913 when President Taft signed into law a bill from Congress establishing the new Cabinet level executive department.
- The National Labor Relations Board was created by the 1935 National Labor Relations Act.
- The Consumer Financial Protection Agency was created by the 2010 Dodd-Frank Wall Street Reform and Consumer Protection Act.

And so on, and on, and on. Each statutory law that creates a regulatory agency or bureaucracy begins by identifying a problem. Sometimes a law will identify more than one problem. The problem might be dirty air or dirty water, unsafe toys, unfair wages at private businesses, or credit card companies that charge interest rates some people find to be unreasonable and "obscene." The problems might be real, exaggerated, or just made up. There might be agreement about how big a problem is, or disagreement. It really doesn't matter.

What matters is that modern, progressive laws 1) identify problems, 2) spawn regulatory agencies and government bureaucracies, and 3) charge those agencies and bureaucracies with solving the problems identified in the laws. Make sense? Identify a problem, then create some bureau of unelected experts to solve it. The actual laws themselves do nothing to solve any problems. Rather, the laws and the lawmakers who wrote them delegate responsibility, authority, and power to solve the problem to bureaucrats like you.

Congress then typically allocates to each government agency a government-approved, taxpayer-funded budget that provides for staff, money, and other resources— along with the legal authority to issue regulations that have the power of law (even though regulations are not actually laws)—all for the purpose of solving the problem(s) identified in the laws. Or, at least, for the purpose of *appearing* to solve the problem(s).

Here's the rub and where you need to pay attention: If you and other bureaucrats *actually solve the problem*, that creates two serious difficulties for your bureaucratic futures. First, there might be no further need for your regulatory agency or bureaucracy. *Quelle horreur!* If the government agency in which you work was created to solve a problem, and you actually solve it—especially if it is a problem that can be solved once and for all—then why should the government agency continue to exist?

Second, even if it's a recurring or on-going problem, which justifies the continued existence of the government agency in which you work, what happens to the operating budget that Congress allocated to your agency or bureaucracy if you practically solve, or almost solve, or greatly mitigate the problem? Your success might lead

Congress to maintain or even cut back on the budget allocated to your agency in future years. Some members of Congress might actually think that if your agency can do a good job, and solve or mitigate problems within a certain budget, perhaps you can be a little more efficient in the future and fix problems with a slightly smaller budget. Do you see how dangerous this path is for you and all other bureaucrats? The very last thing in the world you want is a smaller operating budget. You don't want less money and fewer resources being allocated to the bureaucracy in which you work—you want more.

SUCCEEDING BY FAILING

So how do smart bureaucrats go about getting a larger operating budget from Congress? Answer: *Fail*. And it's usually not sufficient to fail in a small way. It's much more effective to fail spectacularly, in giant ways that the whole world can see. The worse your failure is, the more impact your statements will have when you testify in Congress that more money is needed so that this kind of failure "never happens again."

After Congress creates a regulatory agency or bureaucracy for the purpose of solving some problem, citizens quickly come to equate *solving the problem* with the agency or bureaucracy that was created to solve it. This virtually guarantees the perpetuity of all regulatory agencies and government bureaucracies.

If the Environmental Protection Agency, for example, becomes synonymous with clean air and clean water, then getting rid of the Environmental Protection Agency becomes synonymous with polluting the air and water.

If the Federal Department of Education becomes synonymous with the education of American children, then getting rid of the Federal Department of Education becomes synonymous with getting rid of education for American children.

If the Food and Drug Administration becomes synonymous with safe foods and medicines, then getting rid of the Food and Drug Administration becomes synonymous with poisoned or tainted foods and medicines.

Do you understand why, politically, it's impossible to get rid of any government agency or bureaucracy? So long as voting American citizens equate government bureaucracies with solving problems and improving the lives of Americans, you need not worry about any bureaucracy or regulatory agency being eliminated. Ever.

Further, bureaucrats like you have another technique at your disposal, to reinforce the connection between government and many good causes, while at the same time punishing American voters who don't support bigger budgets for regulatory agencies and bureaucracies. You can deprive Americans of access to places they want to go that don't need government supervision but have it anyway.

For example, in 2013 there was a temporary shut-down of the federal government, caused by members of Congress being unable to agree on a budget. In response and as a way to punish voters, bureaucrats at the National Park Service closed off the entire National Mall in Washington, D.C. Millions of American tourists were outraged that they could not climb the steps of the Lincoln Memorial or walk near the World War II Memorial. Even though neither of these memorials require any government personnel to be on site, the mere experience of being blocked from visiting them caused many voters to demand that Congress pass a temporary, and expanded, spending bill to fund regulatory agencies and bureaucracies. Which Congress quickly did.

See how it works? As a bureaucrat, you not only don't have to listen to what voters want, you can punish voters and teach them a lesson when they vote in ways that don't support your big government, big budget, bureaucratic agenda.

Whenever elected officials are bickering about approving bigger budgets for regulatory agencies, bureaucrats can deny citizens access to national parks, trails, and all kinds of land, buildings, and facilities they control. That's why it's important that bureaucrats control as much land and as many facilities as possible, as if the bureaucrats own it, even though all of it is technically the property of the American people.

SHOW ME THE MONEY

The only important question, then, for each and every bureaucracy and regulatory agency, is: Will its operating budget be bigger next year, the same, or smaller? Even Congress has limits on its resources. Unfortunately for bureaucrats, there's only so much private property and wealth that Congress can take from productive Americans, and Congress can only commit the next generation to repaying so much debt. Congress has to prioritize how it spends resources because all resources—even other people's money—are limited. (Hard to believe, I know.) This means that a rare Congress member might occasionally look for ways to cut back on, or at least not increase, spending for a particular government program and the bureaucracy that manages it so that Congress can increase spending on others programs and bureaucracies.

You want the bureaucracy where you work to be on the list of agencies having future operating budgets increased by Congress. The way you do that is twofold:

First, you and other bureaucrats fail at the core purpose of the agency for which you work. If your agency is tasked with cleaning air and water, for example, see that air and water stay polluted. Or get more polluted than they used to be. If you're in charge of stopping the trafficking and use of illegal narcotics, help distribute illegal narcotics or, at least, turn a blind eye to their flow. If your government agency is supposed to make sure

Americans have access to safe medicines, make sure Americans stay sick or die because they cannot get medicines that might help them. Put up roadblocks, obstacles, and delays wherever you can.

Second, go to Congress and explain in great detail that your bureaucracy or regulatory agency has failed because it lacks sufficient resources. These testimonies are even more effective when you bring large reports filled with charts, graphs, and lots of numbers. Make sure to present the reports in professional-looking plastic covers or binders, as well. These make your reports look much more serious. And...bureaucratic. In addition, bring individual victims of your failures to testify, in person. The more tragic their story is, and the more pain they suffered because of your bureaucratic failures, the more moving their testimonies will be in helping you to get the bigger budget and increased power you deserve.

Throughout this process, you have to exercise and practice failing. Don't underestimate the challenge. It's hard work. You'll have to train yourself to resist the natural impulses of your mind and body. Everything natural within you will push in the direction of excellence, achieving goals, improving yourself, and encouraging others around you to improve as well. You must resist. If you are going to have a long career as a bureaucrat, you *must* resist.

Leave subjects like winning, achieving goals, surpass-ing expectations, producing excellence, learning, and improving one's own performance to non-bureaucrats in the competitive private sector. Leave those things, in other words, to the entrepreneurs in the world of business. Leave those subjects to people who compete to win. It's not your concern. You are a bureaucrat.

Your concern should be singularly focused on failing. You should always come up short. Disappoint others. Don't improve. Don't innovate. Show up late, leave early. Do less than the minimum that's required—you cannot be fired, remember? Stand by as others get hurt and suffer. Because then, and only then, can you complain to your supervisors and members of Congress that you must be given bigger budgets, more money, more resources, and more authority in order to solve the problems your bureaucracy or regulatory agency is charged with solving.

CHAPTER 13

YOUR INCENTIVE FOR CORRUPTION, ER, CRONY "PARTNERSHIPS"

Earlier, in Chapters 9 and 10, we examined two ways that government regulations are valuable for businesses, especially big businesses. First, regulations create quasi-monopolies for big businesses by driving smaller competing businesses out of business, or by preventing new start-up businesses from ever being formed. Often, representatives from large corporations sit down with government regulators and actually help write regulations that will assist the large corporations while piling burdens onto smaller competitors that don't have those inside crony connections and are not involved with drafting regulations.

Second, regulations protect big businesses from taking responsibility for their actions. When large corporations cause damage or harm, they simply claim that they were following government regulations and thereby shift all responsibility from themselves to the bureaucrats who regulate them.

There's a third way that government benefits certain businesses: *subsidies*.

The very premise of a business is that it will produce products and services and trade them for money, or perhaps other products and services offered by others. When other people value the products or services that a business is producing and agree to the terms of a proposed exchange—which usually means paying the price offered by the business—that business is likely on its way to being profitable, barring any unusual circumstances.

When, however, people do not value a business's products or services, that business is in trouble. Or when people prefer the products or services or prices offered by competing businesses, that spells trouble for the losing business. The owner likely faces a difficult choice: improve the products and services her company produces, or lower the price—or improve the products and services *and* lower the price—or go out of business. And many businesses do the latter; they shut their doors and close forever when their costs exceed their revenues for an extended period of time. According to both *Forbes* and *Bloomberg*, eight out of ten entrepreneurs who start new businesses fail within 18 months. That's an 80% failure rate for start-up businesses.

WHEN PEOPLE DON'T VALUE YOUR BUSINESS, GET A SUBSIDY

There is, however, another way made possible by government. When a business cannot make a profit by selling the products and services it offers because people don't want or value them, a business doesn't necessarily have to improve its products or services. Or lower its prices. Or shut down. A business that produces things no one wants can continue to operate—it might even be able to *increase* the price of its products and services—if that business can get a taxpayer-funded subsidy from government.

Every subsidized business—and there are many of them, large and small—is a business that cannot be profitable, cannot generate revenues from sales that exceed costs, and cannot remain open based solely on market demand for the products and services it offers. And that's okay. We're not here to judge, right? This chapter merely illuminates and clarifies yet another incentive that motivates the choices and behaviors of bureaucrats.

For many business owners, it's much easier to land a government subsidy than it is to do all the work necessary to improve products and services enough that customers will value them. And clearly almost any business owner would prefer subsidies, and staying open, if the alternative is closing down.

Taxpayers are the losers in this scenario when the government takes their money and redistributes it to businesses that don't provide value for customers. The losers also include consumers who can't find the best products or services, but merely the products and services that are subsidized. Often businesses that produce better quality products and begin with a sizeable market share find themselves at a great disadvantage against competitors offering lower quality products that are subsidized. But, again, that's okay.

In terms of the taxpayers who subsidize failing businesses that cannot compete in a market, we shouldn't shed any tears for them. Citizens who pay taxes, especially those who pay most of the taxes, are the wealthy. They are the 1%. Well, maybe not the 1% exactly, but they tend to be at the top of income brackets.

- The top 1% of income earners and producers, for example, pay almost 40% of all income taxes.
- The top 5% pay 60% of all income taxes.
- The entire bottom 50% of income earners and producers pay only 3% of all income taxes.

Why only 3%? Because that's their fair share, of course. Why would anyone expect half of the tax-paying United States population altogether to pay any more than 3% of income taxes? When adjusted for transfer payments received from government programs, the bottom 50% of income earners are "net recipient households," meaning they get from government more than they give to it.

THE WEALTHY OUGHT TO PAY THEIR FAIR SHARE

Those in the top income brackets and those who are the most productive tend to be greedy and selfish—that's *why* they're wealthy and why they're in the top income brackets. So it's no great injustice if the greedy and selfish share some of their wealth with struggling businesses, right? In fact, it not only is not an injustice to take from the greedy, wealthy few and give some of their wealth to favored, failing businesses in the form of subsidies, it's fair. It's the right thing to do. It's an investment in those struggling businesses. Using other people's money. Based on choices made by those in government. Who did not earn the money. How could that be wrong?

The important question for you is: How much do businesses value the subsidies they're receiving right now or the subsidies they might qualify for in the future? The answer is: potentially, very much. And *there* is the incentive for you to advance your career through "public-private partnerships," or what is cynically called "crony corruption" by your political enemies, conservative critics of the modern bureaucratic-regulatory state. That's why, every time you hear conservatives and populists accusing you or other bureaucrats of "corruption," you respond by describing it as a "public-private partnership."

For many businesses, the question of whether to pursue government subsidies is a basic financial calculation. Which is cheaper—trying to keep a business going via sales, marketing, and perhaps even innovation, while competing against other businesses, or trying to land government subsidies?

Suppose, for example, some business is going broke. Suppose it's a business that sells environmentally friendly, "green" energy. Suppose it began with investors who put money into the business. But they soon learned that generating green energy is so inefficient and expensive that the business cannot make a profit selling energy at market prices, especially when competing against non-green energy businesses that offer energy that's more reliable and in greater abundance, all at lower rates.

The green energy business might calculate that it will require billions of dollars in research and development, spread out over many years, to produce green energy—wind, solar, what have you—efficiently enough to make it a competitive business model. It might be two decades or more before an investor sees a return on her money. For the green energy business owners, it might make sense to spend significant amounts of their own money to land a government subsidy, especially if the subsidy can begin immediately, rather than try to improve the business enough to be competitive and offer products at prices that customers will buy.

In other words, for some businesses, there's big money to be gained and time to be saved by receiving government subsidies. Which is why they'll *spend* big money to get government subsidies.

This process of businesses spending money to get subsidies from government used to be called "bribery," but now it's known by its more progressive name: "lobbying." Getting taxpayer-funded subsidies from government for private businesses is such a big industry that there are legions of professional lobbyists. Ironically, they're regulated and controlled by bureaucrats like you. Lobbyists have to get licensed by bureaucrats. That's right, these professionals who specialize in getting taxpayer money from government for failing businesses are licensed by the very government they lobby. In Washington, D.C., for example, lobbyists representing all kinds of businesses from all kinds of industries have offices on K Street, just down the road from Capitol Hill. And their location is no accident.

Conservative critics of modern regulatory government call it "cronyism" when government uses its monopoly on legalized power and taxpayer money to help some favored businesses—usually those that give big donations to government officials—and not others. But the term "crony" is so negative that it's a good idea for you to avoid it. What others call "cronyism" is, in reality, an opportunity for you. It's an opportunity to form "public-private partnerships" between government and certain businesses that support expanding government and increasing the budgets of bureaucracies and regulatory agencies.

Often a business must qualify and be approved before it can receive government subsidies. The process of a business being approved for subsidies includes dozens of applications, reviews, and inspections by bureaucrats. If you happen to be one of the bureaucrats in charge of those applications, reviews, and inspections—if you hold the power of determining whether a specific business will qualify for a subsidy—then you become highly valuable to the business owners seeking the subsidies. They might offer you money (directly or indirectly), friendship, invitations to fancy parties, and all kinds of others benefits, if you expedite their applications and approve their businesses as qualified for government subsidies. This is a wonderful opportunity for you to supplement your regular income and expand your social circle of friends while doing good work as a public servant.

Those same business owners who might slip some money your way to help grease the wheels of bureaucratic approval are often busy lobbying elected officials at the same time, especially members of Congress. Hardworking members of Congress typically need and appreciate money from lobbyists because their work requires moving lots of money around for all those in business who expect favors from those in government. Here's a quick guide to how it works:

1. Members of Congress need lots of money to get re-elected and to get assigned to a Congressional committee that has power and influence over businesses. A typical member of Congress must pay about $500,000 to be appointed to an A-level Congressional committee, such as Ways & Means or Energy & Commerce, and $1.5 million or more to chair the committee.

2. Lobbyists will give large sums of money to members of Congress in return for government subsidies for the businesses and industries they represent (as well as all kinds of other perks, including waivers and exemptions from government regulations, tax breaks, and increased government harassment of their competitors).

3. Many of those same members of Congress vote on the budgets for the bureaucracy or regulatory agency in which you work.

You have a vested interest in lobbyists giving large sums of money to help the members of Congress who help your bureaucracy or regulatory agency. It's good for your career, and your paycheck. You have a vested interest, therefore, in making sure the work you do as a bureaucrat helps the businesses and industries that help the lobbyists who help the members of Congress who help your bureaucracy or regulatory agency. Got it?

You also have a vested interest in hurting or punishing any businesses that do not support the bureaucracy or agency for which you work, or who do not support the members of Congress who vote to increase the funding of your agency. And you should always be on the lookout for businesses interested in "public-private partnerships" with government. Let them know that you can help navigate the complexities of government bureaucracies (because you're a bureaucrat and you know the labyrinth of bureaucracies like a rat knows the sewer system), which will be remunerative for you in the long run.

CAMPAIGN FINANCE REFORM

The self-reinforcing process of government regulating and subsidizing businesses, and then businesses, in turn, wanting to influence government regulations and subsidies by means of campaign donations and other money offers, is yet another advantage of crony partnerships for bureaucrats and others in positions of government power. It's perfect, actually. What begins with an increase of government power, and then triggers businesses to spend more money on politics, ends with...another increase in government power. All in the name of "campaign finance reform."

It's no coincidence that every major campaign reform law in U.S. history has been connected directly to surges in government power over and subsidies for businesses. The Tillman Act of 1907 was bound up with the progressive movement; the Hatch Act of 1939 came on the heels of the New Deal; the Federal Election Campaign Act of 1971, amended in 1974—one of the most sweeping attempts to implement government control over campaign financing—followed the Great Society. Most recently, the McCain-Feingold Campaign Finance Reform Act passed in 2002—which was signed into law by President George W. Bush, who acknowledged that it was unconstitutional as he wrote his name on it—reflects the fact that modern government in the United States regulates and/or subsidizes virtually all American businesses in all industries.

All of these campaign reform acts are variations of those in government controlling how citizens spend their own money because some think others spend too much on political campaigns. It certainly is true that spending on campaigns and politics has shot up over the last century. It makes sense. As government increasingly regulates and subsidizes how people do business, people in business develop a deep interest in influencing those who make the regulations and offer the subsidies.

Do you see the delicious irony of how this works in your favor? Consider: Government officials and bureaucrats become more involved in more businesses. Citizens then respond by speaking out and spending their own money to influence those involved in politics and government. They want the subsidies. They want to get exemptions from regulations. Those in politics and government then turn around and say they need to restrict how Americans engage in politics, further regulating the lives and controlling the property of citizens, because there's allegedly too much money being spent in politics and on campaigns. All of which requires that you exercise more power and more control over others.

There's really no question about this. To understand it, one need simply ask: Why would a business throw precious and limited capital at elections if government was neither regulating nor subsidizing that business or the industry in which it operates? What would be the incentive for a business to blow money on political campaigns if there was no possibility of any kind of political crony return? If government was neither regulating nor subsidizing an industry, why would a business choose to spend capital on elections rather than, say, research and development of new products, enhanced marketing efforts, or expanding a sales team?

The truth, of which few are aware and fewer will admit, is that the more power and control bureaucrats exercise over businesses and citizens, the more citizens clamor for bureaucrats to exercise yet more power and control over businesses and citizens. The whole system of government by bureaucracy is designed so that every result is in your favor and expands your power and control over others.

CHARITIES: MONEY-LAUNDERING MADE EASY

Don't forget that many crony charitable organizations, especially those that get all or most of their funding from government, are not only "public-private partnerships," they're also effective disguises for useful money-laundering operations. Here's how it works: A charitable organization is created to provide some service, product, or outreach. Maybe it's women's health services. Or education about the environment. It really doesn't matter what the purpose is, so long as it's publicly respectable.

The charitable organization then applies to government for taxpayer-funded grants or subsidies, receives millions of dollars in taxpayer-funded grants and subsidies, and turns around and gives millions of dollars of taxpayers' money back to political organizations and politicians who support the bureaucracies that provide crony favors, grants, and subsidies to the organization. How else can that be described *other* than money-laundering? The politicians get the money they need to win elections and stay in office, the money-laundering charity gets to continue providing some services that some people find useful and that disguise the money-laundering activities, and it's all paid for by unsuspecting taxpayers.

As just one example, while she was a United States Senator, Hillary Clinton supported ever-increasing, taxpayer-funded subsidies for Planned Parenthood.

Planned Parenthood then turned around and gave millions of dollars to help Hillary Clinton when she ran for President (and other politicians who vote for more taxpayer-funding for Planned Parenthood). See how it works? And all along, Planned Parenthood and its supporters could say with a straight face that the real purpose of Planned Parenthood was not to launder money for Hillary Clinton and other big government politicians, but rather to provide health care services for women.

The trick is that the voting public and, more importantly, taxpayers can never know about this money-laundering process. Some taxpayers think that government agencies and bureaucracies are already too big. Other taxpayers don't like or don't value the charities and businesses that receive big government grants and subsidies. Those taxpayers might become unhappy, even angry, if they learned that their tax dollars help to ensure the perpetuity of regulatory agencies, government bureaucracies, and select crony charities and businesses of which they don't approve.

The best way to hide this important process is to say nothing, ever, about the crony relationships that charities and businesses have with elected members of the government and unelected bureaucrats. Rather, highlight, emphasize, and publicize the *mission* of the crony charities and businesses. Especially if they aim to provide health services for women, or shelters for the homeless, or green energy, etc., emphasize their good intentions. And never, ever, let it be known that these crony charities and businesses are money-laundering organizations that benefit elected members of government and unelected bureaucrats, all funded by unsuspecting taxpayers.

Your knowledge of this system and your skill in navigating it are of great value to you now. But they become even more valuable after your government pension program allows you to retire at an early age. Upon retirement, you are in a great position to become a consultant to the businesses seeking "public-private partnerships" with government. You can collect your retirement and at the same time have the highest paying job of your life working as a business development professional and creating new partnerships between politicians and bureaucrats in government and select, favored businesses.

That is your incentive for forming partnerships. Pay no attention to the Constitutional cranks and conservative populists who call it "corruption" or "cronyism." They're jealous because you are a bureaucrat, and they're not. They're haters. And as every civilized person knows, haters are going to hate. It's what they do. Don't let the hate of petty, envious, conservative non-bureaucrats deter you from the good work and opportunities in front of you.

CHAPTER 14

SATISFYING YOUR DESIRE FOR POWER TRIPS AND ABUSING AUTHORITY

T his is going to be one of the most direct, frank, non-sugarcoated chapters of this book—and that's saying something as the rest of the book is pretty direct, frank, and non-sugarcoated. At first, this chapter might even seem a bit brutal, it's so honest. The way a session with a therapist can be. Gaining honest self-understanding is no easy thing, after all. But you need to be clear and up front with yourself about your desire for legitimate, or at least legally authorized, power over others, and opportunities to abuse that authority. It'll help you get the most from your career in a government agency or office.

Step back, calm down, and breathe deeply. Count to ten, slowly. Clear your mind of distractions. Don't continue reading until your body is perfectly relaxed and your mind is focused. Now ask yourself: *Why did you want to be a bureaucrat?*

Just to make this exercise a little more comfortable, let's trot out the usual answers:

- You want to help others.
- You especially want to help children. You always want to help children.
- And the poor.
- And women.
- And racial minorities.
- And members of the LGBTQ community.
- You want to stand up for those who can't stand up for themselves.
- You are a people person.
- You are not greedy like those who work for private businesses.
- You are a patriot, sort of, when that term is qualified or defined in a progressive way.
- You believe in law and order. And regulations. Lots of regulations.
- To keep others safe.
- To help others flourish.
- Because you want to help others. Sure you do.

Now, after you've repeated those usual answers and you're feeling good about yourself, let's try it a second time: Why did you want to be a bureaucrat? And this time, dig a little deeper into your soul, if you still have one. Dig for a more honest answer. Be genuine with yourself. Be authentic. Know yourself, truly. What about an unelected government job most attracted your attention?

You know the answer. Don't be shy. Don't try to fool yourself. The world is a scary place. There's lots of uncertainty. There are dangers all around us. And in a world of fear, what do you most want and need to feel better protected? *Power.*

It's okay. Don't feel bad. Don't feel guilty. Just be honest with yourself. The goal here is for you to understand yourself. This exercise is about you knowing who you truly are, what you truly want, what you truly need, and how your job as a bureaucrat can supply those things.

GOVERNMENT: THE ONLY REAL MONOPOLY

Now step back, again, and ask: What is government? By exploring this question, you might better understand why you were and remain attracted to being part of government in the role of an unelected bureaucrat.

Government is *the* monopoly on legalized force. Private citizens, who are not part of the government, can initiate force against others, compelling others to do (or not do) something by use or threats of sheer physical power. But their use of force against others is typically in violation of the laws. Those citizens risk punishment because their actions are criminal. Those who are part of government and represent the authority of government, however, can exercise force against others, make others do what they command, and their actions are authorized by law. See the difference? It's the difference between going to jail and putting others in jail.

In fact, government is the only real monopoly, anywhere, ever. All monopolies begin with the monopoly on legalized force. Wherever you find a business, for example, that appears to be a monopoly within a particular industry, look closer and you'll find that that business has a close connection to and protection from government— because only government and its monopoly on legalized force can prohibit or prevent the emergence of competition.

To help you understand how government is the monopoly on legalized force, consider the academic discipline of democide. Democide is the study of governments murdering their own people, directly or indirectly. Democide does not include governments killing the civilians or soldiers of other regimes, such as in war. Rather, social scientists conducting democide research look only at governments that cause the deaths of their own civilians.

In the past century alone, governments around the Earth have slaughtered between 250 million and 300 million of their own people. These numbers include men, women, and children who have died in killing fields, concentration camps, and gulags, as well as people who died from government-caused famines, economic crises, and shortages of life necessities. These numbers of government-caused deaths are inexact and not easy to nail down because not all regimes keep accurate accountings as the corpses pile up. Still, the number of civilians killed by their own governments in the past century far exceeds the number of civilians and soldiers killed by enemy governments, at war, during that same period of time. One's own government during times of relative peace is a greater, deadlier threat than foreign governments during wartime.

All of these civilian deaths that constitute democide spring from governments controlling the lives, property, education, and businesses of citizens. Curiously, the governments that have the most blood on their hands are not ancient; they're modern. Many of them continue to exist today. Ironically, the governments that have caused the most deaths among their own people are governments that have pledged to provide free housing, free food, and free health care for everyone. It turns out that promising free things requires great government power used to control and confiscate, which can lead to terrible, widespread poverty, sickness, and starvation, as well as gross abuses of authority, as dissenters are sometimes persecuted, tortured, imprisoned, and even executed.

It's a strange twist of modern politics that after a century of unprecedented totalitarian tyrannies, many people today blame those tyrannies on "hate." It's not unusual, for example, for holocaust museums and anti-genocide campaigns to emphasize that widespread murder, torture, and starvation result from widespread hatred. But that's far from an exhaustive explanation. Human beings have been hating other human beings since the beginning of human time. Hate alone does not cause millions of people to be rounded up and sent to death camps or starved on barren farm fields. Remove limits on government power, however, and then widespread human slaughter and starvation become possible, because only governments build concentration camps and legally take food from the people who harvested it. Government *is* the monopoly on legalized force.

Not everyone looking to work as a bureaucrat has the soul of a murderous tyrant, of course. Most bureaucrats are nice people, as a visit to any local DMV or Social Security Administration office will prove.

Those who are most attracted to careers in government, as bureaucrats, however, do typically have a desire for power over others. That's *why* they're attracted to government agencies and bureaus. Bureaucrats are the kinds of people who want to control others. There's no shame in that. Often, bureaucrats were bullied as children. Or they had controlling or abusive parents. Or they were the victim of a crime. Or they had lovers who cheated on them. It's okay. Whatever happened to you, it was not your fault.

Bureaucrats, in other words, tend to be people who have experienced pain and suffering at the hands of others. That is why, later in life, they become almost desperate for control over others. And for those who want control over others, there is one institution uniquely and specifically designed for that purpose: government.

In an almost perfectly symbiotic way, it's good that bureaucrats tend to be those who most want and need to control others, because government is the perfect place for them to be. Government needs people just like them. There is nothing comparable to the monopolized, legalized power that comes with a government title. If two ordinary citizens have a problem with each other, for example, there's not much either one can do to the other without violating the laws and getting into trouble. They can talk, resolve their differences, and come to an agreement, or not. But law-abiding citizens cannot force anyone to do anything. What about a conflict between an ordinary citizen and a bureaucrat? That's very different. Imagine, for example, that a business owner does not like the local government building inspector. And the building inspector does not like the business owner. And the business owner needs a permit from the local inspector in order to add ten spots to the parking lot outside his store.

What bad thing will that business owner say or do to the local government building inspector? Answer: Nothing. What kind of force will the business owner use against the building inspector? None. The business owner, even though he doesn't like the inspector, might actually offer him respect or something else of value, maybe even a bribe, to get the permit. The business owner will suck up to the inspector any way he needs to, because he needs the permit. The business owner in this scenario has virtually no power at all.

The bureaucrat, however, has enormous power over the life, property, and future of the business owner because the bureaucrat represents the government's monopoly on legalized force. The bureaucrat can command the business owner to do many things, and the bureaucrat can prohibit the business owner from doing other things. And if the business owner resists or even complains, he might end up in court or even in jail. There's no question, in this scenario, about who is controlling whom.

A bureaucrat is in the perfect position not only to exercise power and authority over others, but to abuse that authority, too, if that's what you're into. Why? Because there are no competitors or alternatives to bureaucracies. Suppose some political conservatives, like the critics who are your professional and political enemies, want to form charitable groups. They need their tax-exempt statuses to be approved by the IRS. That means if you are one of the bureaucrats at the IRS, you have almost complete power over those groups. You have leverage over them, while they have nothing over you. What are they going to do, after all? If they don't like the way they're treated by IRS bureaucrats, to whom are they going to turn for tax status approval? Are they going to get approved by one of the IRS's competitors? The IRS has no competitors.

Because you work for a bureaucracy, you have no customers. You also have no competitors. You may treat people nicely if you like. But you don't have to. You may be mean. Rude. Harassing. Punishing. Torturous. It doesn't matter. You are a bureaucrat who cannot be fired and whose pay rarely depends on how you treat people or what they think of you (except for your supervisor). The possibilities for abuses of power are almost limitless. Isn't it great?

As a bureaucrat, you have at your disposal not only millions of pages of regulations you can use to harass, intimidate, and make life miserable for your fellow citizens, but, more importantly, millions of pages of *contradictory* regulations. As you memorize these regulations and how they require contradictory things, you become a master in the art of personal harassment and destruction. You know exactly when to apply a little of this regulation, when to pull back, when to step up, when to press other regulations. In your bureaucratic hands, the mountains of contradictory regulations become weapons you can use with skill and grace against those you don't like. You're a samurai using a katana. Demand that a business owner complies with Regulation A, and as soon as he does, at great expense, pull out and enforce Regulation B, which requires the exact opposite.

To help your studies, here are some examples from testimony provided for the Subcommittee on Commercial & Administrative Law, which is part of the Committee on the Judiciary in the United States House of Representatives:

- One bureaucrat commanded a Baltimore sausage factory owner to wet mop his floor every two hours. Another bureaucrat told him the floor must remain dry at all times.

- An EPA official directed a hospital administrator in Ohio to purchase a special incinerator for infectious waste. The administrator placed an order, but before delivery, other EPA regulators forced the manufacturer of the incinerators to stop all deliveries pending a regulatory review of their products. The hospital administrator could not acquire the incinerator because of the actions of one set of bureaucrats and thus faced a fine from another.

- The Exxon Corporation reaped public scorn and billions of dollars in fines and cleanup costs after one of its tankers hit rocks in the coastal waters off Alaska, causing a giant oil spill. The company, critics said, should have known better than to allow a man with a record of alcohol abuse to pilot a ship. Later, Exxon was sued for violating government regulations about employment discrimination when it fired a tanker engineer who had a drinking problem.

Those inside government bureaucracies have known for many years that each and every political topic that comes up as the latest, worst problem that only government, allegedly, can solve has virtually nothing to do with government actually solving that problem.

Recall from Chapter 6 that results don't matter. Whether it's the challenge of reducing the gap between rich and poor by making the rich poorer in the name of "fairness," or promoting affirmative action and government welfare programs in the name of "civil rights," or enlisting children in government-managed schools in the name of "free education," or socializing medicine in the name of "free health care," the real purpose of all those political campaigns and the government policies, programs, and regulations that result is to increase the power and authority of bureaucrats. In reality, every political topic offered to the public as a problem for government to solve is a disguise, an excuse, a justification for government bureaucrats to control the lives and property of American citizens. That's important for you to know, as a bureaucrat, because it's key to expanding your power and control.

One recent example of a problem that government offers to solve is perhaps the grandest, most sweeping, most all-encompassing in modern history: global climate change and everything that affects it. You will do well to understand the politics of that subject because climate change activists are key to helping you expand your power and authority, as a bureaucrat, whether those activists know it or not.

THE BUREAUCRATIC POLITICS OF GLOBAL CLIMATE CHANGE

It is a measurable, objective, historical fact that where and when people use fossil fuels they live longer lives than people who do not use fossil fuels. Human beings have been healthier, wealthier, safer, and generally more comfortable since fossil fuels were discovered than they were before.

Yet, for many climate change activists, fossil fuels are like terrible beasts to be slain. At any cost. That is the source of the growing conflicts between climate change activists and entire industries that have been inseparable from modern human progress: the industrialized extraction, refinement, marketing, distribution, sale, and use of fossil fuels.

Inventive human beings have found all kinds of applications for fossil fuels, from reliable generation of heat and electricity, to the growing of foods and development of medicines, to the transportation of goods to stores conveniently located near the people who need them, to the materials used in making the smart phone that's likely distracting your attention right now. And much, much more.

Fossil fuels have become such a large and integral part of our lives that it's no exaggeration to suggest that most people today, at least in developed nations, cannot imagine a world without fossil fuels. The incredible human progress that has been made possible by fossil fuels, however, is routinely ignored altogether by those stoking the growing political pandemonium and demands for increasing government power to combat global climate change.

A MATTER OF BELIEF

In the public arena of mass opinion (where politicians get elected), the subject of global climate change has been reduced to simplistic, soundbite, binary alternatives. One either believes in climate change or not. Real, actual climate change, of course, involves far more than over-simplified matters of personal belief. Still, as a bureaucrat, you benefit when complex subjects can be reduced to simple slogans that mock anyone who disagrees with your agenda. And if you can back up the slogans with scholarship that appears academic—even better.

In a much-cited 2016 essay, several researchers argued that "[t]he consensus that humans are causing recent global warming is shared by 90%–100% of publishing climate scientists…which is consistent with the 97% consensus reported" in yet another study. This is the basis for the oft-made claim that "97% of scientists agree."

Information is trickling into the public realm that reveals how skewed the funding is in the arena of climate science research. Bureaucrats like you have made sure that lots of government research grants are available for scientists who advocate for expansions of government power in the name of climate change. Scientists who question the political agenda of expanding government power receive little or no funding. Could those facts influence the 97% statistic? Perhaps.

More to the point: Reading that much-cited 2016 essay can be a very useful exercise for researchers and academicians and, most importantly, for bureaucrats. It's a model of a political agenda wrapped tightly with what appears to be rigorous "science"—numbers, charts, footnotes, even a bibliography. Dissecting that essay should be homework for bureaucrats looking to expand their power base justified by a cause backed by "science." In fact, it's your homework after you finish reading this book. Find that link and other useful references online at speakeasyideas.com/swamp.

When you start to read that essay, notice little subtleties such as how the authors looked at many research papers that contained *no* statement on anthropogenic global warming, or AGW (a fancy term for "humans cause global warming"), and proceeded to lump those papers together with others that did contain affirmative statements regarding AGW. That's right. Scientists who said nothing about humans causing global warming were lumped in with scientists who said humans cause global warming. Why? Because apparently when scientists say *nothing* about humans causing global warming, that's evidence that they think humans cause global warming. Cute trick, eh?

Whether the number is 97% or not, certainly there's no denying that some scientists agree that human beings influence the climate. How could humans not influence the climate, after all? Curiously, however, this study, which is widely circulated and referenced, is silent on the fact that scientists disagree widely on *how much* human beings influence the climate, *how serious* the problem of human-caused climate change is, and whether *there is any climate change emergency or not.* The authors simply brush over these inconvenient facts because these facts don't help the cause of increasing government regulatory power. Which is why you, too, should brush over these facts.

Finally, when we get down to brass tacks on whether bureaucrats can manage the global climate—whether bureaucrats have the ability to make the climate do whatever they want it to do—there is no consensus among scientists. At all. Why would there be? Why would scientists have faith that bureaucrats can manage the world's climate when bureaucrats are in a line of work where results don't matter? No scientist, likely, will be surprised when the global climate continues to do what it's been doing for millions of years, even after bureaucrats are granted regulatory authority over it. But highly scientific research papers simply don't mention that.

The global climate changes. Always. Endlessly. Denying that the climate changes is like denying your own aging. Your face will have more wrinkles at 55 than it did at 25. These are facts. Suck it up. Those who don't believe their face wrinkles with age or don't believe the climate changes are choosing wishful fantasies over reality.

It is also true that human beings influence the climate. They have to. If mere human observation of phenomena influences the phenomena being observed, which modern physics has discovered, then certainly other human activities influence the world around us in many, and possibly far-reaching, ways. Which leads to important questions. How much—or to what extent, exactly—or in what ways, precisely—does each human activity and the sum of all human activities influence the many variables that, combined, constitute "the climate"? Are human beings in impending, immediate, catastrophic danger from climate change?

These are disputed questions. There is consensus among some, but certainly not all, scientists. (Among scientists, let us not forget, often it is the one or two who disagree with the rest who end up discovering the next great breakthrough in science.) Scientists have achieved little consensus on questions of the precise climate-related dangers we face, including the scope, scale, and timeline of those dangers. The global climate is an amazingly, infinitely complex system within a finite space. It's hard to know with any precision the causal relationship between a change in one climate variable and thousands or millions of other climate variables. With each iteration of change, a process that gets repeated *ad infinitum* within the Earth's climate, the entire climate system transforms into something different while its complexity increases. The Earth's climate today is not what it was a 1000 years ago, 100,000 years ago, or 1,000,000,000 years ago.

HOW WILL THE CLIMATE BE CONTROLLED?

Here we begin to see that many of the most important questions pertaining to climate change are rarely if ever raised in public, and never answered in any satisfactory way. You, the bureaucrat, should keep it that way. You should keep these questions out of public discussions, as best you can—perhaps by using and maybe even abusing some of the government power you have—because questions related to the competency and intentions of bureaucrats distract from the larger purpose of increasing power for bureaucrats.

Here's another example of the kind of question you should keep far away from public and political discussions: How, exactly, will bureaucrats control the infinitely complex system of the global climate?

Many climate activists seem to think that controlling the climate requires controlling human beings and their property, presumably by expanding the regulatory power of government. That's good news for you, of course. But controlling human beings and how they use their own property only goes so far. It still leaves much unanswered. Even if all human beings, everywhere, are brought under strict regulatory control, even if bureaucrats run everything and individual freedom is snuffed out entirely, the climate will continue to change. It always changes. It always has and always will. The climate was changing before human beings walked the Earth. The climate will change when human beings are long gone from the Earth. So how, exactly, can bureaucrats control the climate, even if they're granted complete power over everything? It's not an unreasonable question, but it's a question that delays increasing power for you.

WHAT WILL THE CLIMATE BECOME?

While climate change activists and the scientists they revere have never demonstrated *how* they will engineer, command, or control a system as complex as the global environment, they've also never made clear exactly what changes they're trying to effect, or what they want the climate to become.

Suppose you and other bureaucrats become the new weather gods. Suppose you are given complete legal control and government power over the weather and everything related to it. And suppose you can make the weather do your bidding. What then? What sort of climate will you create? What sort of climate do you prefer? No tornadoes, year-round temps in the mid-70s, rain only after sunset and morning fog gone by 8 o'clock, as a song from the musical *Camelot* suggested?

More human beings live longer and healthier lives right now than ever before in recorded history. The climate, as it is today, seems very good for human life. Should that be your goal, as a bureaucrat in charge of the climate? Do you want a climate that's advantageous for human beings? Or for polar bears? Or red-eyed tree frogs? Or something or someone else?

Which species, if any, do bureaucrats favor? Are present species preferred, perhaps unfairly, over past or even future species? Should dinosaurs be given another climatological chance? Should we focus on the here and now? Or would that be a discriminatory act of present-ism, preferring the here and now over the past or the future?

I hope you are paying attention, grasshopper bureaucrat. Do you see how difficult these questions become? These questions can ruin your opportunity for unlimited power over unlimited numbers of people in the name of regulating and controlling the entire global climate. Questions of what the world's climate *ought* to become and to whom climate conditions should be tailored are not questions that science can answer. These are questions answered by choice, or preference. Not science. Do you understand why you should use any power at your disposal to shut up, shut down, or discredit anyone who raises these kinds of questions in public?

Be warned: If you are accused of geologic discrimination (discriminating in favor of one set of geologic conditions over others), then you will become trapped inside the impossible moral conundrum of recommending and demanding that climate change be controlled and directed by bureaucrats like yourself, on the one hand, without being able to say that any one set of climate conditions is better or worse, superior or inferior, than any other conditions. Stay far away from the quagmire of philosophic relativism: insisting that something (like bureaucratic control of climate change) is good while insisting that "good" is mere perspective or arbitrary opinion.

WHO WILL CONTROL THE CLIMATE?

Finally, if the climate is to be controlled, and if there's any possibility of knowing what the climate ought to become when it is controlled, one question still remains: *Who* will control the climate?

This is the least discussed part of the climate change conversation because it's the most political part. And it's the part to which you must be most sensitive.

You might have a great desire for more power over others, but you don't want others to know about your desire. Rather, you want the American public to think that it is their idea for you to have more power over them. Wait until they insist that your bureaucratic powers be expanded in order to control the climate, and then you reluctantly accept it.

If you are patient and clever, the entire climate of Planet Earth will become the domain of bureaucrats and regulators and you will take your seat alongside the controlling lords of the world. Think about it: Each and every human choice, every human action and inaction, affects the global climate in some way, directly or indirectly. If you are someday in charge of the climate, you will find yourself in charge of everything and everyone. And you will finally have the complete control and power and authority you've wanted your whole life, perhaps to a degree you've never before imagined. That's what is ultimately at stake in the politics of global climate change, though you'd best keep that a secret from the activists and your cheering advocates because they likely don't know it.

CHAPTER 15

PASSING THE BUCK: WHY ELECTED POLITICIANS LOVE UNELECTED BUREAUCRATS

W ithin the modern field of political science, an entire sub-discipline is devoted to studying independent government regulatory agencies and the bureaucrats who work within them. One of the main questions these Ph.D. social scientists study is: *Why do elected politicians create independent government regulatory agencies?*

Many political activists tend to assume that the cause associated with a government agency, in government marketing materials and public propaganda, is the reason lawmakers created the agency. For example, many environmental activists assume that lawmakers created the Environmental Protection Agency for the purpose of ridding our air and water of pollutants. Many educational activists assume that Congress chartered the Department of Education to educate children. Many labor activists assume that the National Labor Relations Board exists to improve the working conditions and increase the pay of employees. You get the idea.

Here, the work of academic social scientists has proven useful, revealing much deeper and well-concealed reasons for the creation and sustainment of independent regulatory agencies and bureaucracies. So if you want to know more about why the bureaucracy where you work really exists, and why it was created, pay attention.

It's no secret that politicians, including members of Congress and United States Presidents, have an interest in getting re-elected. And they're good at it. Political incumbents have re-election rates that average between 90% and 96%. That's right: Virtually every elected member of government who seeks re-election *is* re-elected. This remains true even though public approval ratings for Congress in recent years have plummeted to all-time lows, with approval ratings sometimes of 10% or less.

What gives? How do politicians get re-elected so frequently when the majority of voting Americans seem unhappy with elected politicians? Independent government regulatory agencies and bureaucracies are a big part of the answer.

First and foremost, politicians create independent government regulatory agencies and bureaucracies in order to shift blame and responsibility away from themselves. Or, to be more precise, politicians create these organizations so that the politicians can take credit for trying to solve problems, and avoid blame when new problems arise. Politicians act as surprised as everyone else when a government agency screws up royally. Or just does nothing. Or otherwise fails to achieve its goals. When a government agency fails, elected politicians can look like they're on top of things simply by announcing that they're going to hold a hearing—even though the most likely result of this will be an increase in the failing agency's budget.

Recall that in Chapters 4 and 12 we discussed how regulatory agencies and government bureaucracies are created by laws that identify some public problem and then charge the respective regulatory agency with the responsibility of *solving* the problem. For the elected legislators and executives who pass those laws, the mere act of passing the laws gives them something to brag about to voters. Politicians can claim that they are actively doing much to solve this or that problem because, after all, they passed a law and created a new agency or bureaucracy.

The beauty of this strategy for politicians is three-fold.

First, no one seems to notice that in creating yet another regulatory agency or bureaucracy, all that the politicians have really done is grant yet more power and control over the lives and property of citizens to government itself.

Second, they can pat themselves on the back for solving a public problem when in reality they've solved nothing at all, and very likely created new and worse problems than the one they claim to have helped fix.

Third, when the problem that sparked the law's creation persists, and voters demand to know why government did not fix it, politicians can point to unelected bureaucrats in the regulatory agency and dump the blame on them or their inadequate funding.

In 2015, for example, when the Environmental Protection Agency spilled more than a million gallons of pollutants into Colorado's Animas River, turning the river bright orange and causing states of emergency for many miles downstream, voting citizens in Colorado and surrounding states were outraged. They demanded answers. They wanted to know why and how government could cause such a terrible environmental disaster.

What was the response of members of Congress, especially those from Colorado, as well as the President of the United States? They called for hearings and pledged to find out what the bureaucrats in the EPA had been doing. Each and every elected member of the government made it very clear to voters that they—the elected officeholders—were not the ones responsible for the pollution. Their hands weren't dirty. Elected officeholders pinned all responsibility on the EPA's bureaucrats. In other words, the EPA served the precise purpose for which it was created: to shift blame and responsibility *away* from elected politicians.

This might sound somewhat scary or threatening for you. After all, you don't want to get tarred with blame when elected members of the government fail to accomplish some goal they promised to voters, right? And, after all, your entire bureaucratic career revolves around failing—so how can any politician demand that you be successful, when you must fail?

Read carefully, because this is important: Occasionally taking blame for the failures of elected officeholders is part of the bureaucratic gig. But it's important to remember all the advantages that come with that gig. In return for being the occasional scapegoat for elected politicians, you will enjoy lifelong job security and ever-increasing amounts of money, resources, and control over other people.

If you're still not sure about all of this, consider the case of the EPA contaminating Colorado's Animas River. Not one EPA bureaucrat was ever reprimanded or demoted, much less fired. Think of how dope that is! If you happen to be one of the bureaucrats at the EPA, you can take measures that help keep the water and air clean, or you can take measures that pollute the water and air. In either case, you keep your job, your rank, your salary, and all the benefits that come with your government job. Because—say it with me—results don't matter.

Further, when voters continued to pressure elected officials to get to the bottom of what happened at the Animas River, those officials promised an investigation, including a criminal investigation. But the United States Attorney's Office, which is part of the Department of Justice, quickly decided to turn over all responsibility for investigating the EPA's gaffe to...the EPA. Yes, you read that correctly. Bureaucrats at the EPA were ultimately charged with investigating the actions of bureaucrats at the EPA.

So, see, even if you had been there, as one of the EPA bureaucrats spilling pollutants into a river, you would not have had much to worry about. You would have been judged, ultimately, by fellow bureaucrats who, as we have discussed, have zero incentive to question or challenge or hold other bureaucrats accountable.

And so it always goes with regulatory agencies and government bureaucracies that cause great damage, or perpetrate great injustices, or otherwise violate the rights of American citizens. No regulatory agency or bureaucracy will ever go away—no agency or bureaucracy will ever be dismantled or abolished. Why? Because each and every regulatory agency or bureaucracy represents the cause for which it was created, as we discussed earlier. In this particular example, many Americans continue to think the EPA is synonymous with clean water and clean air. Nothing will ever shake them from that belief. And so long as many Americans maintain that general fantasy—that each good cause is inseparable from the government agencies and bureaucracies created to help the cause—it means a permanent place for you to work.

If you, therefore, in certain emergency situations, have to take the blame for the failures of elected politicians, it's well worth it. It might be uncomfortable temporarily, but it will pass. Sometimes, in moments of crisis, when government fails, the names and faces of bureaucrats are made public. This is unfortunate, to be sure. The good news is that it rarely happens. Almost always, bureaucrats, no matter what wrongs and crimes they might commit, no matter how spectacularly they might fail, remain faceless and anonymous to the public. This is an important institutional design of government bureaucracies, because even though a bureaucrat might be accused of wrong-doing one day, very soon he or she will be right back at work controlling citizens—which is so much easier for bureaucrats when their past wrong-doings remain unknown to the people they're controlling.

If you find yourself in the challenging position of being "named" in some scandal, whether you are at fault or not, another feature of public service can come to your rescue. The vast majority of bureaucratic vacancies are created by an experienced bureaucrat being promoted to a higher position. The vacancy created by the promoted bureaucrat is nearly always filled by another bureaucrat, usually the next person down on the org chart. This continual motion means that if things are uncomfortable for you at one regulatory agency or bureaucracy, where perhaps you were named as part of some scandal, you can quickly and easily move to another agency. Usually with a promotion. And a pay raise. Hence the black eye you received at one bureaucratic office stays at that office, and only temporarily, while you move away from it and get on with your career at a different bureaucratic department, division, or agency.

There is another reason, mentioned in Chapter 13, why elected politicians love regulatory agencies, government bureaucracies, and the bureaucrats who work in them: As the numbers of regulations grow and grow and grow, beyond the comprehension or understanding of any single person, business owners subject to those regulations become increasingly desperate for help. Many businesses simply cannot afford to be in compliance with all the regulations that might be relevant because they cannot afford to hire entire teams of employees to do nothing but study regulations and fill out forms.

These business owners, in desperation, will call or visit or send a lobbyist to their elected representative in Congress. Maybe a business owner will even email the President of the United States. And what do these business owners most want? Relief from the burdens of government regulations. They need help. Or they want special favors. They might ask for an exemption from this burdensome regulation, or for a subsidy that will help them be in compliance with another regulation. Perhaps they hope to persuade some regulatory bureaucrat (maybe you?) to simply forget to track their compliance reports.

When business owners desperately want help from elected members of government, their desperation creates a source of power for those elected representatives. Because now the elected officials are in the awesome position of sitting back, scratching their chins, and deciding whether they want to respond to the pleas for help with a "yes" or a "no."

Elected politicians will make strategic political calculations about whether they want to help, hurt, or ignore a particular business owner. That decision is, of course, always connected to the question of whether a business owner has helped a politician stay in office or not. When favors are doled out, when exemptions or waivers or subsidies are granted, when inspections are cancelled, when reports get "edited," when relief of any kind is made available to select businesses, those favors and that help will come through *your* office, because you are the bureaucrat working inside the bureaucracy that regulates, controls, and often crushes businesses (or at least the ones that don't get crony favors and exemptions).

In other words, in the process of politicians increasing their power by effectively torturing business owners with impossible regulations until those business owners beg for mercy, you play a vitally important role. You are the one who actually makes all of that happen. You make the promises of favors and perks and special treatment for select businesses become real.

This is yet another important reason why politicians *love* the work you do as a bureaucrat. Elected politicians *need* you. You are indispensable for their growing base of power over the lives and property of other people. So even if now and then you find yourself getting blamed for the irresponsible failures of said politicians, know that your reward will come as those same Senators and Representatives will never consider eliminating or even scaling back the regulatory agency or bureaucracy where you work. No one in government will ever consider firing you or in any way tampering with your career as a bureaucrat. It's the kind of reward that no one else can receive except for bureaucrats like you.

PART
IV

PRIVACY:

THE DEVIL'S DEN

CHAPTER 16

CATEGORY 4 CHOICES: THE GOVERNMENT'S RIGHT TO CHOOSE

As your training continues late into the book, we are going to return again, briefly, to the older, Constitutional view of government that evolved during the American Founding, and contrast it with modern regulatory government. In particular, let's remember that Constitutional government was predicated on the distinction between the public realm and the private realm. The older view was that all legitimate government power granted for the proper purpose of government—protecting individual natural freedom and private property—was to be exercised over citizens in the public realm, or when they come in direct contact or have direct interaction with each other.

The old view held that Constitutional limits placed upon the power and authority of government were a recognition of a realm of privacy, or what some call the *right* to privacy. We protect the private areas of our lives from government interference by placing clear Constitutional limits upon the power of government, thereby prohibiting government from entering and regulating the realm of privacy. That realm of privacy under a limited Constitutional government used to include family life and how parents raised and educated their children; religion and what preachers chose to say or not say from their pulpits; politics and how citizens voiced and published their opinions about elections, and which candidates and policies they chose to support and in what ways; and how a business owner ran her business and who she chose to hire, fire, and what products and services she chose to offer and at what prices. The realm of privacy, under limited Constitutional government, used to be expansive.

In fact, under the Constitution that Americans used to follow, the entire economy was considered to be in the realm of privacy. Whether the national economy was growing or shrinking, doing well or doing poorly, was a matter for citizens to worry about, or not, because earlier generations of Americans recognized that the "economy" is really the sum total of private individuals' work, production, and trade with each other, locally and internationally. Supply, demand, wages, prices of products and goods, and more belonged to the realm of privacy. The government had no business and no legitimate Constitutional power to stick its nose into the economy.

Hopefully, as a budding bureaucrat who has made it through so much of this book, you've come to understand that the basic ideas of government regulations, and the bureaucracies created to implement regulations, and the bureaucrats who enforce regulations, are premised on a *rejection* of the distinction between the public realm and the private realm. This premise is important for your career. Modern government regulations are founded on the belief that there is no realm of privacy, no right to privacy—except, perhaps, the right to abortion, the Constitutional foundation for which features an argument defending the right of privacy. Other than abortion, however, the premise of regulations is that the whole of human life is *public*, from the foods people eat, to the medicines they take, to the books their children read, to the kinds of safety seats into which their children must be strapped, to just about everything else. All areas of human life are public, and therefore all areas of human life should be regulated. By you. And other bureaucrats.

The bureaucratic rejection of the distinction between the public and private realms creates great opportunities for you. It creates great responsibility, too. Sometimes it'll feel like your shoulders alone are holding up the entire world. Be reassured by the fact that as a bureaucrat, you're never alone. Where there's one bureaucrat, there are thousands close by. Millions, actually. Like with gnats and mosquitoes.

Also, don't ever underestimate the great education and training that prepared you for such responsibility. As was pointed out in the Introduction, your university degree in Women's Studies, or Queer Theory Studies, or Multicultural Studies, the volunteer work you did decorating "safe spaces" with brightly colored blankets, pillows, and comfortable chairs, and the protests in which you participated while holding signs you borrowed from your roommate and chanting slogans you didn't understand will have you ready and able to control all areas of the lives, property, education, health care, and businesses of others.

The right to privacy is the right to nefariousness. When people have access to a private realm, they use that privacy to hurt, steal from, deceive, or bully and belittle others. What most people do in private is just no good. Which is why progressive civilizations don't allow privacy. The realm of privacy truly is the Devil's den. The realm of privacy is the preferred home of bigots. It's the space where supreme selfishness does its work, tempting people to do nasty, vicious, and downright mean things to each other. The more we can minimize, restrict, and regulate the realm of privacy, and the more we can treat every area of human life as public and subject to control by bureaucrats like you, the better we, society as a whole, and the world as a whole, will be. Social progress is synonymous with eliminating the realm of and right to privacy. Leaving you in charge of everything, because once privacy is gone, everything that remains is in the public realm and subject to your control.

PRIVATE VERSUS PUBLIC CHOICES

One way to understand better why privacy offers such great temptations for bad human behavior is to examine the kinds and qualities of choices people make Below is a Matrix of Choices made famous by the economist Milton Friedman.

CATEGORIES OF CHOICES

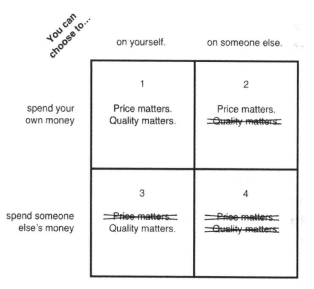

In Category 1 of the Matrix, we see that, typically, when a person makes a choice to spend her own money buying something for herself, she cares about and pays close attention to both the *price* and the *quality* of whatever she is purchasing. Why? Because it's her own money she's spending. And, she's the one who's going to own and use whatever she's buying.

As we move to Category 2, however, things start to change. When a person spends his own money buying a product or service for someone else—a gift, for example—he tends to care less about the quality, because he won't be owning or using it. But he does care about the price, because, again, it's his own money he is spending.

Category 3 presents the scenario of someone buying something for herself using someone else's money. Why worry about the price when someone else is footing the bill, right? A person making a Category 3 choice wants the best quality she can find because she will be the one who owns and uses the product or service being bought, but she won't care at all about the price. Because she's not paying for it.

Category 4 encapsulates the results when someone purchases an item with someone else's money that will be owned and used by yet another person. Stated differently, Category 4 represents Person A choosing how to spend Person B's money on something that will be owned and used by Person C.

Where does one find Category 4 choices? Government. Every choice government officials make, both elected politicians and unelected bureaucrats, is a Category 4 choice. Routinely, they choose how to spend other people's money, never their own, on yet other people.

For example, when elected politicians provide subsidies to American farmers, all of which are shepherded through the U.S. Department of Agriculture by bureaucrats, they are spending other people's money (taxpayers' money) on yet other people (select farmers who qualify for subsidies, according to the professional judgment made by bureaucrats).

Professor Friedman had the arrogance to suggest that choices made in Category 1 are somehow superior to choices made in the other three categories. In particular, he was very outspoken in his judgmental opinion that choices in Category 4 tend to be the worst quality choices, simply because people are spending others' money rather than their own.

Pay no attention to Professor Friedman's opinions. His statements can be dismissed, and even excused to some degree, based on the likelihood that he had little awareness of his privilege as a white cisgendered male in the United States. Additionally, he probably failed to take into account historically marginalized groups or the study of victimhood, so his words and ideas and arguments should be taken with several grains of salt, to say the least. He was an economist and, like most economists, he held the shallow view that only data, facts, and evidence matter in the academic pursuit of knowledge, ignoring the very real feelings of other people. We should pity him, rather than trying to show why his ideas were so bad and unfair.

Still, his Matrix of Choices deserves some commentary simply because it's become influential in small political circles of people with peculiar views about government, especially cranky Constitutionalists and other conservative critics who rail against big government bureaucracies. As a bureaucrat, and given the education you've likely had and your professional experiences, you might not know that there are some Americans who do not adore and worship government. But it's true. There are American citizens—a decreasing number, thankfully—who actually question whether it's wise to continue increasing the size and scope and power and resources of government. A few delusional Americans actually think that not every human problem should be addressed by creating new government programs or expanding existing ones. They're your political enemies. As a reminder, an important purpose of this book is to help you refute or at least dismiss those critics through mockery and ridicule.

Critics of big government are weird people, to be sure. Sometimes dangerous. Those who question or challenge government programs and policies are the people who should be at the top of every government terrorist watch list, and for good reason. Bureaucrats like you absolutely should be monitoring and even spying on American citizens who question whether bureaucrats should have more money and power and control. After all, those kinds of Americans are a threat to your career, so what could be more important than watching them when they don't know it, and keeping tabs on everything they do, while erecting as many bureaucratic obstacles in their lives as possible?

These quirky but dangerous critics of big government are the kinds of people attracted to Professor Friedman's arguments and his Matrix of Choices. The good news is that these people don't have many friends and are not very influential—I mean, *come on!* Still, if you could help to change a few of their minds, it'd be good for you simply because the fewer critics you have, and the fewer people who are asking questions about or challenging what you do professionally, the better.

CATEGORY 4 CHOICES

What Professor Friedman presents in Category 1 is the realm of privacy, where selfishness and greed and vindictiveness and hurtful intentions run rampant without any regulatory control or bureaucratic oversight. Category 1 is where one finds the oppressive source of capitalism, including unfair wages, unfair income gaps between the rich and poor, unfair income gaps between men and women, unfair income gaps between white people and non-white people. Category 1 is where individuals calculate what to do with their own resources and their own wealth and their own productive labor that exploits the vulnerability of others. Category 1 includes individuals who discriminate and actually choose *on their own*, without any regulatory oversight, with whom to do business, where to shop and spend their own money, and to whom they offer their products and services. That's what Category 1 choices are all about.

Category 4, on the contrary, is the realm of the public interest. The common good. Category 4 represents choices made without personal interests or selfish motives involved. Yes, there might occasionally, rarely, be an instance of some less than honest politician making a bad choice about spending taxpayers' money in Category 4. But those are the exceptions, not the rule.

In general, when politicians and good, decent, bureaucrats like you make choices about how to allocate, spend, and use other people's money, those choices are made with the interests of other people in mind. And the common good. They are choices made with a view to serving society in the best way—because everyone wins when society wins, right? Category 4 choices are made according to elaborate, scientifically designed budget processes that ensure the wealth and resources produced by some people actually get to those who most want and need them. They are choices that make things fair and keep people safe, which is the grand purpose of your career as a bureaucrat.

So let no one disparage or mock Category 4 choices. Help your fellow bureaucrats learn to become effective teachers with the ability to persuade critics of government that what we most need, as a society, in order to make real social progress, is not more Category 1-type individual choices. What we most need are more collective choices, like those in Category 4. As that happens, as Category 4 expands, the public realm expands, so people are safe and happy and things are orderly and predictable. Why? Because the public realm is highly regulated and controlled by you and other bureaucrats. As Category 1 shrinks, the selfish and hurtful realm of privacy will shrink too, until hopefully, maybe, someday, the problematic realm of privacy is gone once and for all.

CHAPTER 17

PRIVATE PROPERTY: THE SOURCE OF ALL SOCIAL ILLS

T his chapter is less practical and more theoretical than the other chapters of this book. My editors and I even discussed whether or not to include it in a "career guidebook."

This chapter offers advanced training and deeper, philosophic education for those bureaucrats who want more than a steady government job. It's for the bureaucrats who want to advocate at a high intellectual level for replacing representative, limited Constitutional government with an unelected bureaucratic-regulatory state. This chapter offers that training and education by sketching out the arguments that demonstrate why the realm of privacy, the right to private property, and individuality, are the ultimate sources of all social ills as well as the biggest obstacles to creating an unelected bureaucratic-regulatory state that controls the lives of subjects without any inconvenient Constitutional limits on government power.

By understanding the philosophic case *against* private property, which corresponds to the philosophic case *for* total government, in other words, you will be better able to persuade others to grant unlimited power to unelected government bureaucrats. Like you.

PHILOSOPHY

In a famous passage from his *Discourse on the Origin and the Foundations of Inequality Among Men*, first published in 1755, the philosopher Jean-Jacques Rousseau summed up the origin of private property and the great social evils that followed:

> The first man who, having enclosed a piece of ground, and to whom it occurred to say *"This is mine!"* and found people sufficiently stupid to believe him, was the true founder of civil society. How many crimes, wars, murders—how many miseries and horrors mankind would have been spared!—if someone had pulled up the stakes or filled in the ditch and cried out to fellow men: *"Beware of listening to this imposter! You are lost if you forget that the fruits belong to everyone and the Earth to no one."*

Rousseau was correct, on two counts. First, private property is in no way natural. It is unnatural. Artificial. Property has no connection to human nature. Property is nothing but a contrivance of human imagination.

Second, every social ill or injustice—from crimes to war to murder, from selfishness to greed to treating others as expendable, from unfair low wages to unfair high prices to unfair interest rates charged by credit card companies, to human-caused global climate change—can be traced ultimately to the idea of private property.

I saved this chapter for near the end of the book because it's a reminder and personal reinforcement for you if ever you begin to question the government work you do. If you find yourself late at night, staring in the mirror, unable to sleep, having doubts about whether you are doing the right thing by confiscating the property of others and controlling their businesses. Or if conservative critics are questioning and challenging the regulatory agency where you are employed. This chapter will help in those dire moments of personal crisis.

Know this, bureaucratic grasshopper: In the end, human beings can never find peace, happiness, and justice until private property is gone once and for all. Until that glorious day comes, whenever it might be, if ever it might be, the best we can do is have bureaucrats like you to regulate and control property as if it is all public, rather than private. Regulate everything as if it belongs to everyone. And that is ultimately why your work and your career are so important.

THE DANGEROUS PSYCHOLOGY OF PRIVATE PROPERTY

Rousseau's teaching—the idea that private property is both unnatural and the source of all social ills and injustices—was adopted and developed by Karl Marx in the middle of the 19th century. Marx, in turn, became one of the great sources of inspiration and learning for the first generation of American progressive intellectuals and academicians in the late 19th and early 20th centuries.

These American progressive intellectuals were the ones who leveled the first serious critiques against the United States Constitution at the same time they were designing the modern bureaucratic form of American government. So you owe a great debt to them. They made your career today possible. They also designed the progressive research university, which has since become the model of modern higher education, and the modern social sciences, including the sciences of "public administration" and "bureaucracy." Understanding the thinkers who contributed to the modern social sciences of bureaucracy and government by regulations will help you understand better the overall purpose and importance of your work.

Back to Marx. He was less a theorist of politics or economics than he was a *psychologist*. His main goal, ultimately, was not merely to analyze or even change politics or economics, or to change laws or policies. His goal was to change the way human beings *think*. Approach him that way, and the pieces of his entire life's work come together.

Marx was interested in how human beings understand themselves and those around them. He wanted to change that understanding. He believed that changing the self-understanding of the human mind was eminently possible because the mind, according to Marx, like all of human nature, is malleable, almost like plastic, to be shaped and formed in new or different ways.

MIND AS MATTER

Marx denied the metaphysical freedom of the human mind. Marx was too sophisticated, too educated, too smart to believe in old-fashioned, outdated concepts like the freedom of mind, or free will, or the existence of free "souls." The mind, Marx argued, is matter and nothing but matter—because the whole world consists of matter, and nothing but matter. Marx was emphatically a *materialist*. He believed that the only reality is material reality, material things, physical matter. Anything that's not physical matter is not real, nothing but an illusion, according to Marx. Anything immaterial is nothing but a fantasy, a myth, a wish, or a dream (or a nightmare), like gods and angels and devils and demons.

The operations of the mind, therefore, or what we might call "thinking thoughts," are mere effects of the material causes around and acting upon the mind. Thinking, in other words, is an *effect* of various physical *causes*. Change the causes, and one changes the effects. Or to state it more cynically: Manipulate the causes of human thoughts, and one can manipulate the content of human thoughts.

If the mind is nothing but physical matter and a function of material cause and effect—if the mind is not metaphysically free from the laws of physics—then mere matter precedes ideas. Mere matter *causes* ideas. The material, physical environment around us causes our minds to form "ideas" of the material, physical environment and the many physical things of which the environment consists. The mind is like hot wax and the physical, material world around us is like a signet ring, leaving behind impressions or representations. Those impressions or representations, from the Marxist point of view, are what we call "ideas" or "thoughts" that represent the physical, material world around us.

This probably seems somewhat abstract, and theoretical. It is. But stay with me. It is important because it provides the theoretical framework for understanding why private property is the source of all social ills, and why your work as a bureaucrat is so important in helping to rid the world of private property.

CONNECTION BETWEEN SELF AND PROPERTY

So where, from the Marxist view of mind and matter, did the idea of "self" come? How did human beings ever become aware of themselves? How or why did they begin to distinguish their own interests, or the interests of "self," from the interests of others?

The answer, according to Marx, is *property*. The presence of physical, material, legally protected property correlates with and causes ideas of "property." From the idea of owning property, it's a short skip and a hop to the idea of having property in one's self, and therefore owning one's self and the fruits of one's labor. And *who* is the being that owns its labor? The self.

This, according to Marx (and Rousseau before him) is the materialist origin of the concept of "self," which Marx saw as the ultimate root of human problems. If we can eliminate the concept of "self," then we can solve all moral and political problems once and for all. Why? Because if we eliminate the concept of "self," we eliminate greed, selfishness, self-interest, and all the social evils that flow from self-centered passions. One cannot be selfish, after all, if one's mind has no concept of "self."

But how can this happen? How can human minds forget the concept of "self?"

Here's how. If material reality precedes and causes all ideas, then a change in material reality changes the ideas held by the mind. This is why Marx was fascinated with the final communist revolution that would abolish all private property once and for all. Privately owned property, in all forms, according to Marx, would be removed from the private hands that claimed ownership of it and, instead, be held in common by the people, the community, the "commune."

WE REPLACES *I*

As the presence of private property is eliminated, so too, Marx argued, the *idea* of property will dissipate. As the idea of property dissipates, the idea of self-ownership dissipates. And as the idea of self-ownership dissipates, the very idea of "self" will disappear from the consciousness of individuals.

Once the concept of self is gone—once there is no "I" to which a man or woman or transgendered person might refer—once all persons identify themselves only in terms of *we*—an entirely new kind of human being will have evolved: the true *communal person*, or what Marxists used to call "The Communist Man." (Forgive their insensitivity to gender identification, they did not know.)

Ancient philosophers such as Plato and Aristotle argued that politics is a permanent human problem that can never be fully or finally solved. They believed this, in large part, because they thought that human beings are political creatures on the one hand—human beings will always be part of some form of a political community. And they believed, on the other hand, that there will always be conflicts between the interests of individuals and the collective interests of a political community.

What some individuals see as good for themselves will conflict, from time to time, with what a community proclaims to be good through its laws and public policies. This conflict between the individual and the collective is permanent, argued the ancients, because individuals will always be conscious of *self*. The self-awareness of one's own self is inseparable from human nature, and human nature is immutable, according to the ancients. That's why, from the ancient point of view, there are permanent human problems, including the political problem.

Marx, however, claimed that he had discovered a solution to the political problem that ancient philosophers thought was unsolvable. With the disappearance of private property, the dissolution of the concept of self, and the emergence of a new *communal personhood*, politics as the ancients understood it—a permanent problem caused by conflicts between individual and collective interests—will cease to exist. Self-awareness of the self will be gone. No one will have any consciousness of individual self-interest because no one will think of themself as an individual. No one will think in terms of "I" or what is "mine." The group, the collective, the communal consciousness of *we*, is all that will remain after the ultimate communist revolution.

For the first time in recorded history, human beings will become total communal beings. And as community becomes the most important thing in human life, there will be no more prestigious occupation than being a community organizer.

YOUR WORK

As a bureaucrat, you likely cannot bring about the ultimate, world-wide communist revolution. Don't sweat it. As a bureaucrat, you're probably plenty satisfied to move from being a GS-12 to a GS-13, or maybe even ascend to the vaunted ranks of the Senior Executive Service. No problem. The typical bureaucratic soul is not looking to revolutionize the world.

Don't lose track, however, of the importance of your work. Even the best Marxist governments need bureaucrats. Lots of them. The common hallmark of great Marxist empires, aside from murdering millions of dissident people (which is forgivable, because their intentions were really good and, as you now know, results don't matter), is gigantic government agencies, offices, and departments staffed by millions of bureaucrats. After all, controlling every detail of the lives and property of millions of people is no small job, right?

The point is that whether you're working inside the United States government as a bureaucrat, or within regulatory agencies and government bureaucracies in other countries, you can do much to transform private property into public property, simply by regulating, controlling, and occasionally confiscating it. These important bureaucratic activities will help to teach everyone under your power that their property is not really *theirs*, that it's not really private property, that their property belongs to you because you represent the power and authority of government.

Here's an example that you can emulate. In 2016, in Chicago, Illinois, a popular bar, which leased space inside a building in downtown Chicago and featured live music, violated the terms of its lease. The building owner wanted to evict the bar and lease the property to another business, which was fully within the legal rights of the business owner. But a Chicago city alderman did not like that decision. So he threatened to change the zoning regulations, limiting to whom the building owner could lease his property. This would've cost the owner thousands, possibly even millions, of dollars. When the building owner complained about the harassment and regulatory control over his property, the Chicago alderman told him to "come back on your knees" when he was ready to renegotiate.

See how that bureaucrat, in that instance, effectively taught the building owner that his property was not really his, that it belongs to government, that bureaucrats will decide, ultimately, how property is used or not in the public interest?

If you do your job well, controlling, regulating, and confiscating what belongs to others, soon you'll notice that increasing numbers of citizens begin to ask you what they are allowed to do or not allowed to do with their own property. This is a sure sign of social progress. It means justice and fairness and equality are starting to replace injustice, unfairness, and inequality.

When citizens ask permission from bureaucrats to do something with their own property, or their business, or their home, or their children, it not only means more power for you, it means citizens are implicitly acknowledging that their property belongs to government, to the community. It means that consciousness of private property is waning. And this is an important step toward getting rid of private property, shrinking the realm of privacy, and forcing citizens to think fewer selfish individual thoughts of "I" and more about the communal interests of "we."

(Note: Even though much of the philosophic background for the lesson contained in this chapter came from Karl Marx, it is highly recommended that you not mention Marx in public or even among fellow bureaucrats. Americans today love the ideas of Marx and Marxist concepts, but they're slightly embarrassed by it, so best not to use his name when you're mingling with respectable company. It's much easier to market Marxist teachings in the United States today by never mentioning Marx.)

CHAPTER 18

A BUREAUCRAT'S WORST NIGHTMARE: TURNING REGULATORY AGENCIES INTO ADVISORY COMMISSIONS

E very now and then we hear about conservative cranks or loud populists who suggest eliminating a particular regulatory agency or bureaucracy. The good news for you is that these complaints are the mere sounds and fury of idiots, signifying nothing. As we've made clear throughout this book, no regulatory agency or bureaucracy ever goes away, for a number of reasons, and bureaucrats don't get reprimanded or demoted, much less fired.

Still, there are dangers. Your political enemies, the cranks, Constitutionalists, and populists, are always scheming to reduce your power.

Remember that while the Supreme Court in general is your friend—both Republicans and Democrats on the Court are quick to grant more power to you and your fellow bureaucrats—and even though the Supreme Court has upheld the Constitutional legitimacy of independent federal regulatory agencies and government bureaucracies, that does not guarantee that these organizations must continue to exist in their current form. As we discussed in Chapter 5, there is no provision in the United States Constitution for any federal regulatory agency. Every one of them was created by a statutory act of Congress, which means those agencies can be transformed, scaled back, or defunded by a simple statutory act of Congress.

Recall that at the federal level, the government includes 15 executive branch departments. Virtually all federal regulatory and administrative agencies and sub-agencies—which number in the thousands, and employ directly around 3 million non-military, civil service bureaucrats—fall under the authority of one of these departments. Should extremists in Congress today wish to get serious about reclaiming the authority of the Constitution, they might begin by rejecting any so-called omnibus spending bill in favor of a real, actual budget. A real budget would include 15 distinct sections, funding each of the government's executive departments separately, that would provide for clear oversight of the way that funding is used/misused by each department and the many regulatory agencies and sub-agencies within them.

That alone would spell trouble for you because it would make it easier for others to observe how much money is being spent by the bureaucracy or regulatory agency where you work.

TURNING REGULATORY AGENCIES INTO THINK TANKS

There is a proposal floating around some political circles of which you should be aware and which you should do everything you can to destroy. The idea is to take away the power to issue arbitrary regulations and thereby transform regulatory agencies into mere advisory commissions or think tanks.

This proposal is dangerously deceiving because it retains (at least initially) regulatory agencies, bureaucracies, and government offices, which makes it appear unimportant and unremarkable to the voting public. But it would remove the power to issue regulations from all federal government agencies, which *is* radical, because the power to issue and enforce regulations is the single greatest power bureaucrats have. Should this proposal be enacted by the United States Congress, it could spell the end of your career. At a minimum, it would turn your position upside down by removing the most important power you have over the lives and property of citizens.

Members of Congress could, if they wanted, pass a law transforming all regulations issued by regulatory and administrative agencies into mere *suggestions* that have no legal force and no legal authority whatsoever unless and until those suggestions are approved by a vote of both chambers of Congress and signed into law by the President. This would effectively strip you of the power to control the lives and confiscate the property of citizens. Rage, rage against the dying of the light!

Could this actually happen? Perhaps. Imagine the nightmare for you if the President, current or future, conducted a series of high-profile, public, televised interviews with directors and employees of various federal regulatory agencies and government bureaucracies, including possibly the bureaucracy where you work. With spotlights shining, microphones on, cameras recording, imagine if a United States President started directing these kinds of questions at unelected bureaucrats:

- Where in the Constitution is the authority for your agency?
- Please explain to the American people why regulations have the power of law when they are not, in fact, laws.
- Describe the actual process, step-by-step, of how unelected, unaccountable, un-Constitutional bureaucrats issue regulations that self-governing citizens must follow.
- How many businesses did your regulatory agency intimidate or harass last year?
- How many businesses did your regulatory agency force to close last year?
- How much do your regulations increase the cost of goods and services for consumers and how

harmful are those higher prices for the poorest Americans?

- How many Americans remain sick, or die, or otherwise suffer because of some product, service, medicine, or technology that could not be offered and sold on an open and free market because your agency would not allow it?

- How many businesses have moved their operations to other countries to escape your regulations?

- How often do your regulations provide an advantage for one business over its competitors?

- How often do you issue exemptions and waivers so that one or more crony businesses don't have to comply with your regulations while their competitors do?

- How often do citizens, including business owners and corporate officials, who are to be the subjects of regulations, advise on the formation of regulations?

- Which kinds of businesses are harmed the most from your regulations, small or big ones?

- How many charities, churches, schools, and other organizations that promote views different than yours has your agency threatened or intimidated?

- What is the budget for your regulatory agency, who pays for the salaries and expenses of your agency, and what rightful claim to other people's money does your agency have?

- How much do regulators and bureaucrats make at your agency? And how do their incomes compare with those of similarly skilled emloyees outside of government?

- How many ineffective, incompetent, or just plain bad employees are you prohibited from firing because of civil service tenure?

- Why are government agencies so inefficient compared to private businesses and organizations?

- Has your agency *ever* achieved its goal or even come close?

Imagine if a sitting President spoke openly to the American people and told the truth that independent regulatory agencies and government bureaucracies and government programs help some people yet, typically, end up doing far more harm than good. What if a President pointed out that government bureaucracies are not and can never be nearly as effective as market forces and open competition among businesses? What if a President made it clear that while some bureaucrats, as individuals, are fine, honest, decent people, still, the very design of regulatory agencies create all kinds of bad and perverse and counterproductive *incentives* for those who work in, and those who have crony connections to, federal regulatory agencies?

Do you see the problem this could create for you? Voting citizens might start to demand that their representatives in Congress do something about the very real problem of unaccountable and virtually unlimited power vested in and exercised by regulatory agencies and government bureaucracies. This would jeopardize not only the power position you enjoy over fellow citizens, it would cut deeply into your ability to grant regulatory favors, waivers, perks, and subsidies to crony business friends. It would diminish your power to harass businesses that compete with your pals' businesses. It would make you less valuable to business owners, which means they'd have little interest in throwing huge sums of money toward you and others in government.

If you had less regulatory power over citizens and their businesses, we would actually see less corporate money being spent in American politics. Think of the many ways this would be bad for you, your supervisor, fellow bureaucrats and regulators, and even the elected officials who authorize the budgets and regulatory power of the bureaucracy where you work. It would be disastrous for bureaucrats and their crony friends alike. Your entire power base is your ability to issue and enforce regulations and have judges pretend that regulations are laws. It's what makes it possible for you to act like a lawgiver, an executive, and a judge, all at the same time, without any danger of being kicked out of elected office (because you're not elected). Yet Congress does have the authority, with a stroke of a pen, to take away the power of regulation from all agencies and government bureaucracies.

And that could happen if a President or someone else brought public attention to the great damage being done by the un-Constitutional, expensive, wasteful agencies and bureaucracies where you and your bureaucratic friends work. Members of Congress could turn your powerful regulatory agency into a mere think tank, where you and other bureaucrats research problems and offer your conclusions to Congress, and make recommendations for legislation for members of Congress to consider. This would mean a complete loss of regulatory power for you, because it would mean no control over the property or businesses or lives of citizens.

Whatever else you do in the course of your career, your number one goal should be to conceal and keep from public attention the waste, fraud, corruption, abuses of authority, harassment of citizens, ways you punish voters, damage to personal lives, crony favors to select friends in business, and above all the failure of regulatory agencies and government bureaucracies to achieve their respective goals. You should repeat, whenever possible, the feel-good fiction that each and every regulatory agency and bureaucracy and program and policy is inseparable from solving the problem it was created to solve. Remind citizens that education is impossible without a Department of Education, that clean air is impossible without an EPA, that wages agreed to by employees and employers would be impossible without a Department of Labor, and that global climate change can never be controlled and engineered without bureaucrats coordinating across dozens of different agencies and bureaucracies. Teach Americans to connect everything they care about with a government program, agency, or office.

And whatever else you do, make sure to remind elected members of the government, including those in Congress and even sitting Presidents, how much their positions of power depend on the crony favors and regulatory punishments they're able to dole out to business friends and enemies, all of which would be impossible without powerful regulatory agencies, sprawling government bureaucracies, and millions of bureaucrats like you, who have the power to control and regulate the property, businesses, lives, and freedom of citizens. Find political groups and organizations that advocate for more bureaucracy and regulations, more government entitlement programs, more subsidies, and single-payer, universal, government-managed education, housing, and health care. Nurture your friendship with them. Find individuals who have big business interests that would benefit from more bureaucracy and regulations, and offer assistance in avoiding the burdens of regulatory compliance. Find people who sing the praises of bureaucrats and regulators, and people who vocally oppose all critics and populists and conservative naysayers who would in any way dilute the bureaucratic power you have over others.

Do whatever you can to prevent the power of regulation from being taken away from where you work. Everything good for you depends on keeping that power and expanding it. It's indispensable for saving the swamp of government bureaucracies and agencies.

THE IMPORTANT WORK AHEAD

H opefully, now that you've reached this concluding chapter, you've come to understand better what it means to be a bureaucrat. You should now know the incentives available to you that will influence the professional choices you make and actions you take. This book has catalogued the many tools at your disposal to exercise and expand your power over others while climbing the ladder of bureaucratic success. All of this material has been organized to help you put your career into overdrive.

Your work is important. Know everything you can about it. It will be good for you. Good for your fellow bureaucrats. Good for your crony friends who need special government favors. And good for the United States of America. (Cue playing of "God Bless America.")

Also, you should have a clearer picture in your mind of who your political enemies are—the conservative Constitutionalists and populists discussed in the Introduction—and the way they think about politics and policies. These critics want to reduce your power and scale back the modern regulatory-bureaucratic state. You have deep professional and personal interests in making sure they do not succeed. This book has taken some brief detours here and there to review the outdated political philosophy of the American Founding and the original Constitution, as well as certain basic ideas of extremist free market economic theory, because many of your critics either take those ideas seriously or they rally around those who speak as if they understand and agree with those ideas.

Throughout this book, you've been provided with practical tips and advice for how best to refute those critics, how to mock, discredit, and dismiss them, and how to change the topic, which is often the most effective way to handle any critique of government agencies, policies, programs, and bureaucracies. Remember, when confronted by challenges to the important work you do, toss out a reference to Hitler, or accuse your opponent of racism, and that usually ends the discussion then and there.

If you want to continue learning, the sources referenced in this book and additional materials are available online at speakeasyideas.com/swamp.

What many Americans today call the "swamp," or "deep state," is nothing dark or mysterious. It's not a bad thing. Rather, it's a wonderfully good thing. The swamp is a network of millions of government employees who have devoted themselves to making sure Americans live their own lives, run their own businesses, use their own property, and educate their own children in ways that make sense. In ways that are planned by scientific experts. It is highly debatable and debated whether the origins of human existence and the universe in which humans live were the result of intelligent design or not. But with your help, and the help of millions of other bureaucrats, Americans today can be assured, without any question or debate, that their future will be intelligently designed. By you. And the many bureaucrats with whom you work.

The future will be intelligently designed, that is, so long as you and others work together to save the swamp. Maybe even expand it by making the swamp wider and deeper, which in practice means more bureaucrats with more power, more resources, and more money being removed from the private hands that earned it and channeled to the growing ranks of government employees, who know how best to spend other people's money.

You are now prepared to advance your bureaucratic career on the fast track, to get ahead, and get more power, more control, more money, while at the same time taking down the critics who question and challenge the bureaucracies that have become the very symbols of American greatness. No one is taking the United States back to the 1950s when selfish business owners ran amuck without bureaucratic oversight and control. Gone are the days when young entrepreneurs with little capital tried to start businesses in their homes and apartments. Never again will people in schools make amateurish decisions about what the educational curricula should be for students. Everyone and everything will be licensed, certified, regulated, controlled, and government approved. Diversity will be replaced by uniform, universal, national regulations and policies to which all Americans will conform. Conformity is the future you will provide for your fellow citizens.

We're not going back to the chaos and social injustice of limited Constitutional government. Free markets are a relic from the unenlightened past. Because you and other bureaucrats will stop those who would turn back the clock to the time of discrimination, bigotry, racism, inequality, and unbridled greed. The future will be determined by bureaucrats, of bureaucrats, for bureaucrats. The future is one of government designs and three-year, five-year, and ten-year plans.

As government agencies and bureaucracies become more secure and permanent, they continue to become more powerful. And more power means you can do what you want, when you want, how you want, with whom you want. Power means freedom, the very thing that you must take from others if you, the budding bureaucrat, are to enjoy it for yourself.

ABOUT THE AUTHOR

Prior to founding Speakeasy Ideas, Dr. Thomas Krannawitter taught at Claremont McKenna College, Hillsdale College, and George Mason University. He holds a Ph.D. in political science from the Claremont Graduate University in California.

He's been studying bureaucratic-regulatory government, what some call the "swamp" of the modern administrative state, for over 20 years. Who's better suited to offer career advice for bureaucrats and regulators than an expert on modern bureaucratic-regulatory government?

The author of several books and countless articles, Dr. Krannawitter's more recent essays and podcasts can be found at speakeasyideas.com. Speakeasy Ideas packages the ideas of wealth creation, production of value, increased efficiency, and human flourishing into easy-to-use educational, inspirational products for business owners, employees, teachers, students, parents, children, and citizens of all ages. None of which is relevant for bureaucrats swimming in the swamp, of course.

One way to show appreciation for a book you enjoy is to share your opinions with an honest review on Amazon.

Made in the USA
Middletown, DE
15 July 2019